EARLY PRAISE FOR *SEASONS OF THE BIRCH*

Can you ever really go back home? In *Seasons of the Birch*, Colonel (retired) Puska's characters face obligation, loss, and resentment as they return to, and sometimes stumble over, their roots after serving in World War II.

—*Elizabeth Kauffman, Retired US Diplomat*

Seasons of the Birch tells the story of the sacrifices an Army nurse and other military veterans made during World War II and highlights the struggles and life adjustments they faced upon returning home.

—*CH (COL) Brian Martinus, Command Chaplain, 46th Military Police Command, Michigan Army National Guard*

Immediately, you feel dropped into the 1940s Upper Peninsula of Michigan and the lives of the women in one family who have suffered joys and pains as they reconcile their desire to leave the area, but are pulled back by the rugged beauty, family history, and questions about what could have been. It's a story about the changing opportunities for women, their families, the place they call home, and our nation during and after World War II.

—*Suzanne Alfaro, International Development Practitioner*

Seasons of the Birch offers a glimpse into the past when nurses of "the greatest generation" served their country in unique and selfless ways. Little did Ruth know the challenges she would experience when she left northern Michigan for service in the Army during World War II and when she returned home.

—*Gwen Worley, Retired Workforce Development Administrator*

A nostalgic look back at Michigan's Upper Peninsula during the first half of the twentieth century that allows readers to accompany Ruth on her journey from childhood to Army nurse to wife and mother. Not only do we experience the natural beauty of the location, but also the struggles and challenges Ruth and others of her generation faced.

—*Kristin Bates, Retired Mental Health Agency Personnel Manager*

Susan Puska's novel is a rarely told story about small-town Americans who came together for a common cause during World War II from different backgrounds, occupations, and races, and then struggled to find their footing after their return. Postwar life was not easy, especially for women and people of color whose skills were devalued despite having served bravely during the war. Yet as they reintegrated into small-town America, they fought another battle to reintegrate and expand options for themselves and others. A must-read!

—*Peggy Simpson, Reporter for fifty years in Texas, Washington D.C., and Eastern Europe, President of the Washington Press Club*

Seasons of the Birch reveals so many untold stories of ordinary Americans. One that stands out is the story of a hospitalized African American nurse, a veteran of WWII. The unequal treatment received by people of color, so eloquently described in this book, challenges us to elevate healthcare for all Americans and put an end to a system that treats one race as more deserving than another.

—*K. David Boyer, Jr., Corporate Director, Truist Financial Corporation*

Seasons of the Birch is a story that needs to be told. The author, Susan Puska, is the perfect storyteller because she grew up with the stories of her parents from World II, the life she experienced growing up, and her own military service to America. This unique perspective provides insight to those who have been forgotten: those on the home front and those who sacrificed to ensure America's resilience and freedom.

—*William Pulsipher, Jr, former Senior Vice President International Operations, ICF, and retired U.S. Army Infantry Officer*

SEASONS OF THE BIRCH

SEASONS OF
THE BIRCH

SUSAN M. PUSKA

NEW DEGREE PRESS

SEASONS OF THE BIRCH

ISBN   978-1-63676-812-0 *Paperback*

978-1-63730-230-9 *Kindle Ebook*

978-1-63730-256-9 *Ebook*

Dedicated to my parents, Ruth and Clarence Puska, and their generation who inspired this story and Carol Yee, who encouraged me to bring it to life on the page.

CONTENTS

———

We never know how high we are
Till we are called to rise;
And then, if we are true to plan,
Our statures touch the skies—

—EMILY ELIZABETH DICKINSON

CHAPTER 1

HOME

(NOVEMBER 1944)

———

Ruth Amundsen closed her eyes. She inhaled deeply, holding her breath as if preparing to plunge into a long underwater stroke. She wanted to imprint the memory of this brisk freshness filling her lungs. With her next breath, she smiled as the perfume of pine drifting up from the forest below engulfed her. Ruth studied the endless stretch of Lake Superior across the horizon to the north. She felt a calming peace, her mind anchoring into this wild place. *Home*, she thought. She wanted to remember all of it, to carry it deep inside her like a talisman to rely on in the uncertain times ahead.

At age twenty-four, Ruth felt behind, like she had already missed out. She wanted to do something exciting, even reckless, to get her life moving forward. A few inches over five feet tall, Ruth stood shorter than her two older sisters, Anna and Linda. Her tiny waist and slim build made Ruth look like she might blow away in a strong wind. Her kind face, the one she showed to friends and strangers alike, lit up with the rising sun. Defying a mysterious facial paralysis that she suffered as a child, Ruth could not help smiling and laughing, as if a light radiated inside her. With dark brown eyes and matching hair, she looked more like Anna and their father, while Linda's lighter freckled complexion and reddish hair made her look like a younger twin of their mother.

Ruth and Anna left Marquette in the morning darkness to reach the Knob near the village of Big Bay before dawn. To Ruth, Big Bay would always be her home: the place where she was born and spent her childhood until the logging business collapsed during the Depression and their father moved his large family, three girls and four boys, to Marquette hoping to find work, but he never did. The village shared its name with the large bay on Lake Superior to its north, but it lay tucked into a corner of Lake Independence, once a swampy area, deepened by a dam built in the early 1930s.

A high, rocky outcrop overlooking Big Bay, the Knob, gave a grand view of Lake Superior. Driving up the bumpy dirt road begged caution that Anna ignored as she raced to beat the sunrise. Ruth felt lucky they avoided hitting any deer, paralyzed by the car's headlights, as they hurried to the top.

After Anna parked the car, Ruth walked out across the rocks, relieved to arrive in time and in one piece. Anna went hiking around the rocks below Ruth. Ruth smiled at the low, orange rays of the rising sun racing west across Lake Superior, warming up the deep chill and promising a day of fluffy white clouds and blue sky to break the dreary chill of November.

"What are you thinking?" Anna yelled, rushing up the rocks like a sprinter racing an imaginary competitor. Her face broke into a broad smile of joy as she leaned into the steep rocky hill, shortening her steps as she ran up the crest with a laugh. Anna's beautiful smile broke many boys' hearts as a young girl. Now at age thirty-six, she still looked youthful and beautiful. She wore sturdy, leather hiking boots, scuffed from long treks through the northern woods and lakeshore around Marquette. As she reached Ruth, Anna gave her a gentle push of the shoulder, as if trying to wake Ruth up from a dream.

Anna wore her favorite outdoor clothes: a multi-sport ensemble she had created years earlier to hike, ski, and snowshoe during the long northern winter months. Her pants of dark-gray wool with fitted legs ballooned out slightly over her hips before fitting snug at the waist. She wore long ragg wool socks that stopped below the knees. Her heavy, navy-blue-and-white Swedish-patterned sweater with matching mittens, a favorite set Ruth had knitted several Christmases earlier, completed her outfit.

"Oh, nothing. I'm just enjoying the air and the view," Ruth said.

"Nothing, huh? Little sister, I should know by now that your nothing holds a lot of something. What gives?" Anna chuckled scrutinizing Ruth's face for a hint.

But rather than answer, Ruth evaded the question by reminiscing. "This is such a beautiful place. Remember how, as kids, we used to hike up here from Big Bay for picnics?"

"Beautiful?" Anna scoffed. "It's ugly this time of year. All the color is gone. It's sad as dirt with all the trees almost bare. You should have been here in early October when the leaves peaked. The color blazed this year."

"You can still see some color flashing in the light. Look: blood-red maple leaves clinging to those branches down there. And, anyway, the white birch trees always stand out in the fall," Ruth insisted, pointing north to spots in the woods.

At the mention of the fall color, Ruth imagined bright orange, yellow, and red leaves: an annual show she loved each fall and missed since she graduated the previous year from nurses' training in Marquette and moved to Detroit to work at the Henry Ford Hospital.

"Those were hardly 'picnics' back then." Anna interrupted her thoughts. "We barely had any food—maybe a boiled egg and a piece of hardtack. And we hiked because we were too poor to have bikes." Anna laughed.

"Yes. But it was good, too, wasn't it? Remember how we hiked all around the woods here and along the water?" Ruth said.

"You have a very odd memory. I remember working like a dog for nothing, and you and poor little Jack pulling that battered red wagon around scrounging through garbage. Garbage! Just to find some food or something to sell or use. Humiliating."

At the mention of Jack, the youngest brother, Ruth wondered where he was now. She seldom heard anything from him. They had been close pals before their mother died. Afterwards it seemed the family frayed apart as the boys escaped to build their own lives and Linda married. As the oldest, Anna tried her best to care for her two remaining younger siblings, but Jack dropped out of school and took to wandering about like the hobos.

Ruth asked, "Have you heard from Jack?"

"I sent him some money a while ago. I don't know where he is now, though. I worry he's living rough somewhere," Anna said.

"Remember when we found that crate of grapefruit?" Ruth smiled. "Jack and I thought it must be good if the hotel served them. And they were, as you may recall," Ruth said.

Anna gave an exasperated sigh.

"Ruthie, what are you doing? Your jacket is wide open. You'll catch your death in this cold," Anna snapped in a protective way, changing the subject.

Ruth wore a wool, navy skirt with matching wool tights that made her legs look long and sleek. On top she wore a new, embroidered, white sweater she bought at Hudson's Department Store in Detroit. Her jacket, a stylish blue-and-white checkered wool wrap-around style fell open, forcing Ruth to hold it together.

"You look like a city gal," Anna said like a proud mother.

Ruth stared ahead, pausing a moment before speaking. Used to sharing everything with Anna, she realized she must tell Anna now before they got to their cousin Eddie's place where it would come out anyway. She turned to face Anna and announced, "I volunteered for the Army Nurse Corps, along with Margaret and some other nurses at the hospital. I report for training in January and should be in a unit by the spring." She spoke with a certainty she did not feel as she considered what lay ahead. "You knew it was just a matter of time. This is my chance."

Anna's face appeared blank: an inscrutable Scandinavian calm. Ruth sensed a mixture of anger and calculation.

Finally, Anna said, "Ah, I knew you were up to something. I had hoped this war would be over before you could do something like this."

You know I would have volunteered as soon as I graduated from St. Luke's last fall if you hadn't stopped me, Ruth thought but did not say aloud, avoiding rebuking Anna.

As if reading Ruth's mind, Anna said, "I stopped you from doing this last year to protect you. You know what they've been saying about women in uniform in the newspapers, and people believe it. I don't like it. It is hard enough being a woman without joining the Army for goodness sake."

"People attack the Women's Army Corps, not the nurses. Besides, they need nurses now, and I'm ready to go," Ruth said.

"Oh, so now they say they need nurses, do they? Last year the military announced it didn't. People even discouraged women from joining, rather than be called whores and lesbians. Let the bastards care for themselves," Anna scoffed.

"They've been recruiting at the hospitals again. They need nurses. That's why I decided to join up."

"There's no changing your mind?" Anna blurted, seeming to try to think of a way to get Ruth out of this. "I don't know what I would do if anything happened to you," she said, softening her tone.

"It's too late. I signed the paperwork. I want to help our boys. There are so many wounded. I'll be all right, Anna. You know I'm always careful." Ruth patted Anna's arm. "Besides, it will be a chance to see something of the world, and with good medical and dental care I can't afford now. I'll also be able to make more money than I can at the hospital so I can buy more savings bonds. Aren't you always telling me to save more?"

"There are easier ways to make money. You could find a position as a private nurse for some rich old man, and maybe end up a rich widow," Anna said, half joking.

"Anna, sometimes I think you have no morals at all. I'm not going to chase an old rich man for his money," Ruth laughed. "Anyway, I'm sure going to miss this place."

"I don't know why. I hate this dump. I can't wait to get out of here. The insurance company offered me the chance to move to Tulsa, and I am going to take it now that you're leaving. There's no reason to stay here anymore with everyone gone," Anna reasoned. "The boys have all scattered and Linda has moved away with Stewart. High time I move away too. It will be a good place for Frank to come home to and from the Santa Fe railroad, instead of coming all the way up to Marquette. I'll see more of my husband that way."

After some moments of silence, Ruth said, "You don't hate this place. Otherwise, you wouldn't keep coming back here."

"Yes, I do. It reminds me of poverty...and Pa. You were too young. You missed the worst of his cruelty. And the reason I come here is to see Eddie and Mary."

Ruth did not reply. Although she experienced their father's verbal abuse and violence during his drunken rages, Ruth could never make up for the fact that she had not suffered the worst like her sisters. Too young and lacking her sisters' beauty to catch her father's eye, she should have felt relieved—lucky. Instead, she felt guilt for being spared.

Ironically, Anna protected Ruth after their mother died, yet Anna's anger always re-surfaced like a broken record stuck in a groove, stinging Ruth. Anna acted like this when she felt anxious, as she seemed to now, knowing that Ruth would be going off to war in a few months, exposing herself to danger and the possibility of being wounded, captured, or even killed.

To change the mood, Ruth said, "At least, we don't have to walk today like we did when we were young since you have a car."

"I will never forgive you if anything happens to you." Anna sighed. They stood in silence for a few awkward moments. Then Anna picked up on the refrain she often nagged Ruth about. "You know, maybe you can learn to drive in the Army."

Ruth smiled, understanding that Anna had only temporarily set aside arguing. Ruth expected to hear more about this, maybe for years to come. "I don't know if they let nurses drive. It seems we would have more important things to do."

"You need to get places just like here," Anna reasoned.

"Maybe, but you don't need to drive in the city, Anna, even in Marquette. You can walk or take a bus or the street-car everywhere. I expect the Army will be like that—taking you where you need to go, otherwise you are marching there. Anyway, you know I couldn't get the hang of it that time you tried to teach me," Ruth retorted, feeling tense as she remembered Anna screaming at her about slipping the clutch until Ruth stopped the car, got out, and insisted Anna drive.

"Driving," Anna continued, "gives you freedom. A gal needs two things if she wants her independence in this man's world—her own money and a car."

"I don't think I'll ever need a car, but I'll keep trying to save money. I hope to save up for my hope chest in the Army. I heard they started to pay women the same as the men based on their rank. Goodness knows there won't be much to buy if I go overseas." Ruth laughed.

As the sun spread across the Knob, Anna and Ruth stood next to each other enjoying nature's show. Anna declared, "Let's head into the village and the cemetery before we go over to Eddie's."

"Let's stay a bit longer. I hate to leave this view. I want to watch the sunrise a few more minutes. We have plenty of time," Ruth said wistfully.

A chilly wind blew up from the lake. Ruth saw Anna's expression change to anger again and felt uneasy. "You know, each time I come here I feel so angry at Pa for squander-ing our land to those rich investors from Detroit and who knows where. They took advantage of the homesteaders to get hold of cheap land to cut down the white pine. Then, after they stripped away the trees, they had the nerve to preserve some of the forest for a private reserve for club members," Anna said.

"We've talked about this. You know Pa never registered that land properly and even if he had, he never could have paid the taxes on it. There's no use thinking about it. At least they hired Eddie as a caretaker, so we can enjoy what remains, even if the family can't own any of it," Ruth responded.

CHAPTER 2

AMONG THE WHITE PINE

(NOVEMBER 1944)

———

After sitting together on the Knob, Anna persuaded Ruth back into the car to continue north to the village of Big Bay and the cemetery where their parents were buried. Anna maneuvered her car down the gravel hill, swerving back and forth to avoid the ruts and puddles from a recent rain. Ruth jumped each time the speeding car threw up a stone with a loud clunk to the undercarriage, which made Anna laugh. As Anna approached the stop sign at the crossroad, she skidded the car into a slight fish tail stop before turning left.

"I wish you wouldn't drive so fast!" Ruth said, hitting Anna hard on the shoulder.

"Ow, that hurt," Anna laughed. "Anyway, I know what I'm doing. Skidding on gravel is no different than stopping on skis. Remember how we use to race down the hills?"

Ruth smiled at the memory, correcting, "You raced. I followed you down. Once we reached the bottom, we hiked back up in the deep snow carrying our skis on our shoulders. Over and over, all day long. How did we have that much energy?" Ruth asked not expecting an answer.

Ruth's mind drifted. She admired Anna's natural athleticism. She excelled at any sport she tried while Ruth tagged along. She felt she never measured up to her eldest sister in any way because after they moved to Marquette teachers said things like, *Oh, you're not as smart as your sister Anna, are you?* Even home economics became a personal trial, as the teacher told her, *You're not pretty like your sisters, so avoid the color red. No need to bring extra attention to yourself.*

But the scrappy kid inside Ruth also recognized she excelled in one sport—gymnastics—which her flexible body seemed made for. Nursing also came naturally to her once she got through the difficult coursework and into the hospital. Ruth even knew she excelled in reading, having studied every word of the dictionary on her own in grade school. And she read all the plays and poems of Shakespeare in an old volume a teacher gave her in high school. Her literary efforts did not lift her grades, but she could out-spell anyone in the family, including Anna.

"And skating across the pond as soon as it froze over until it got mushy and dangerous: remember that?" Anna continued her reminiscing. "I have no time for games these days. Too old and too much work to do at the office. Anyway, Frank doesn't like exercise, or nature, unless it comes with a dry martini and a cigar."

Ruth laughed, hearing the truth in Anna's joke. In an odd way, Ruth found Frank Tremblay a good fit for Anna, even though they seemed to have little in common. Anna read books. Frank read newspaper headlines. Anna loved the outdoors. Frank preferred hotel lobbies and elegant bars.

Anna enjoyed a friendly game of cards. Frank seriously gambled during his off time while working on the trains between Marquette and California, often winning then losing it all. They did share a love of gourmet food, Frank's passion, which exposed Anna to fine dining. And Anna, who never drank alcohol, learned to enjoy mixed drinks before and after dinner, a habit Ruth found worrisome and surprising since hard liquor had fueled their father's abuse. When Ruth expressed her concern though, Anna dismissed it. *Oh, I can handle it. I'm not like Pa*, she claimed, but Ruth wondered.

"Odd. Not many people about on a Saturday, and it's almost 10 a.m.," Ruth exclaimed as they drove past the Lumberman Tavern, built of wood scavenged from a school in nearby Birch after the mill closed in the 1920s.

Anna slowed down as they reached the center of the village: a collection of random buildings left over from the last lumber boom. The dry goods store, always stuffed from floor to ceiling with anything from candy to fancy dresses to machinery, stood like a set from an old Western movie with a wooden overhang held up by trees as poles.

"Not many people at any time anymore," Anna replied. "Not like the old days."

Further down the road, Ruth smiled at seeing the Presbyterian Church she'd faithfully attended each Sunday with her mother before they moved to Marquette. *Not Lutheran, but not Catholic*, her mother said, deciding it was better than nothing. Ruth learned to pray there for better days and the strength to deal with the ones she had in the meantime.

Across the way stood the Burns School: not the one Ruth attended that burned down in 1936, but a passable replacement. As a young girl, Ruth peeked through the windows of the school where her older siblings studied in a multiple grade classroom until their teacher, Mrs. Specter, grew tired of sending Ruth back home to her mother. She allowed Ruth to stay inside if she would sit quietly. For another child that might have been a challenge, but at age four, Ruth already learned how to sit quietly and listen. She loved to be around books and neatly drawn letters, eager to learn how to read.

Ruth recalled one day the teacher read *The Ugly Duckling* to her while the older kids worked on their homework. Ruth listened intently, feeling the story held an important message. It offered hope that although both her older sisters seemed better than Ruth, maybe she was a swan. It made her want to read the words herself.

"Blink and you'll miss it," Anna scoffed. Ruth ignored her, thinking how peaceful the village looked, a great place to play as a child, running around with her pals, Eddie, Jack, and Joe. Her older sisters and brothers never seemed to have time to play with her, but she enjoyed a sense of freedom in their neglect. Even the knowledge that she had to watch out for black bears did not dampen the adventure.

The road forked ahead. The left side went toward the cemetery and the Mountain Lodge compound beyond it. The right side wound around the north side of Lake Independence. Straight ahead Ruth noticed the Big Bay Hotel. "What's that?" she asked.

"Old man Ford is having that fixed up as a private hotel," Anna answered.

Anna drove on to the village cemetery, parking at the entrance. Neat rows of wooden crosses and headstones marked the graves on both sides of the sandy road as they walked midway into the cemetery, stopping at an open spot near the side of the road. Ruth felt a chill as the wind blew in from Lake Superior. She pulled her coat tight around her as they stood in silence looking at the ground, the scent of pine drifting over from the tree line that surrounded the cemetery. Ruth placed a bouquet of dried flowers on her mother's unmarked grave.

Cautiously, Ruth appealed, "You know, I have some money now. Why don't we go in together to buy a headstone? Ma's been dead for almost fifteen years. I hate it that nothing is here to remember her by. Isn't it time we forgave her? She did her best for us, and she was too sick to do anything about Pa at the end. We should forgive her." Ruth ached in sympathy for their mother. Ruth remembered when she became too weak to knead bread, allowing Ruth to help by standing on a box to reach the table.

"No!" Anna yelled. "You are not spending the little money you have on that grave! I forbid it."

Ruth sighed. They'd argued over this so many times since their father died a few years back. When he lived, he shirked his responsibilities, claiming he had no extra money for their mother's headstone, hoping to shame their mother's side of the family into buying it. He reacted violently—screaming and swiping at anything or anyone within his reach—when asked about his wife's missing headstone. Now that he lay dead next to her, the missing headstone lurked like a ghost. As the oldest, Anna became the main stubborn obstacle to putting up a headstone for their parents, or even just for their mother. Ruth felt sad that Anna could not forgive their parents. Not for the first time, Ruth saw their father's personality flash in Anna sometimes.

They stood in silence as Anna clenched and released her fists over and over, her mouth tight with anger. Ruth knew not to touch or talk to her when Anna boiled like this in case she lashed out, so Ruth waited several minutes, then said, "Anna, let's go. Eddie and Mary are expecting us."

"Let's go," Anna repeated absently, as if she just realized it herself. They returned to the car and Anna, still brooding, slowly left the cemetery as the road changed from gravel to hardpacked sand. Anna remained silent, clenching her jaw as she drove through shallow puddles, indifferent to the mud splashing up against the car.

When they arrived at the entrance to the compound, they found the gate locked. Anna blew the car horn. Ruth rolled down her window, remarking about a new Huron Mountain Lodge sign, but Anna remained unresponsive. Staring into the compound while they waited, Ruth relished the vaulted medieval forest of towering trees surrounding them. The dirt road, an ancient trail long cleared of undergrowth, snaked its way ahead, running parallel to the shore of Lake Superior. Pine needles and leaves covered the road like a natural quilt. The intoxicating fragrance of the forest took Ruth back to treks with Eddie, Jack, and Joe, as they ran along the nearby trails to the beach.

Soon a figure dressed in a red and black checkered hunting jacket with matching cap, its ear flaps flying loose above his ears, approached the car. Eddie Amundsen smiled and waved as he unlocked the gate. His angular features, dark eyes, and dark hair made some doubt his Scandinavian roots, but like Ruth, he had been whitish-blond as a child.

"You made it!" he yelled to them as he opened the gate to let them drive in. "You know where to go." He motioned to Anna to drive behind a cabin hidden by a grove of trees as he locked the gate behind them.

Anna parked behind the cabin: a roomy structure set back into the surrounding woods that stood close enough for Eddie to monitor the entrance and walk the property, but distant from the client cabins closer to Lake Superior. They got out of the car just as Eddie arrived. He gave each of them a quick hand to the shoulder and grabbed their overnight bags, carrying them up the stairway into the cabin.

"How was the road? Did you see any deer? Mary's waiting for you. She been cooking for days." He spoke in rapid bursts, not waiting for responses, as he led the way up to the cabin. A quiet, thoughtful man, Eddie sometimes rushed through a recitation of his stored-up ideas and questions all at once as if he might forget them otherwise.

"Eddie, give them a chance to catch their breath. You'll have plenty of time to pepper them with questions." Mary laughed as she stood holding open the door. A tall woman, Mary wore wool slacks and an open flannel shirt over a long underwear top. "Come on in out of the cold. It gets so cold under these trees."

"Yes, let's get out of the cold into the cabin and drink some coffee. Mary set up the extra room," Eddie said.

Anna pushed ahead, stomping her way up the stairs, signaling that her anger about the headstone had not cooled. Ruth ignored her, pausing to look up into the white pine towering above the cabin, almost falling backward as she strained to see the tops of the trees, taking in deep breaths of their fragrance.

"Eddie, you're the luckiest man in the world to live in these woods."

"Don't I know it. Come inside."

"Eddie, put the bags in the guest room," Mary commanded as they entered the cabin. Then, addressing Ruth, Mary said, "Anna beat you to the bathroom." She paused before continuing. "Ruthie, you're skin and bones. You always were such a tiny gal. You look quite smart in that outfit, though. You put us country folk to shame." Mary laughed, grabbing Ruth into a big hug. A gregarious Irish woman, Mary had a full laugh and electric smile. She counterbalanced Eddie's more somber personality.

The smell of a wood fire mixed with the smell of coffee, thimble berry pie, and freshly baked bread greeted them. Mary kept the cabin neat and tidy. She decorated it in an eclectic style, combining pieces of driftwood and rocks from the beach with knickknacks the rich club members discarded. Eddie and Mary enjoyed rescuing, repairing, and reusing castoff items, like the Chinese statue Mary had carefully repaired. It stood in a place of honor on a bookcase.

The original owner of the cabin had built it in the 1920s. Then he modernized it in 1940 with the latest features, including a spacious bathroom and up-to-date kitchen. Eddie and Mary moved in a year later after the owner built a more luxurious cabin near an inland lake on the property and the club decided to convert the cabin into the caretaker's quarters.

Ruth studied the centerpiece of the large, open living and dining room: a floor-to-ceiling fireplace made of lake stones. A partial loft behind the fireplace overlooked the entire room. The interior walls of shaved logs with white chinking in between gave the room a rustic look. Smaller logs and branches, also stripped of their bark and finished with a clear coat of varnish, magically transformed into multiple comfortable chairs and love seats. Around the exterior walls, shelves of neatly ordered books—a legacy of Mary's time as a librarian—filled the walls and table nooks.

"This room always makes me feel so happy and warm," Ruth said to Mary, who was fussing around the large oak dining table, laden with more food than Ruth knew they could eat over a week, let alone one meal.

"You made it just in time for a little coffee," Mary said inviting Ruth to sit down. "Let's eat and then you can walk with Eddie along the old path worn through the woods to the shoreline while I prepare supper."

"This is hardly a little coffee—you have a full meal here. I'm sure this will be enough to tide us over until tomorrow," Ruth laughed, not surprised to see how much Mary had prepared.

"Nonsense," Mary replied. "You can never cook too much food."

"Anna, that's one fancy car you're driving. An Austin, eh? Is it new?" Eddie interrupted as Anna walked into the room and joined them at the table. Ruth noticed Anna must have splashed water on her face to hide her private tears. Ruth felt a pang of sympathy mixed with frustration that Anna could never forgive their father for being a monster, or their mother for her failure to protect her girls. Ruth wanted to transcend those dark years. *We all need to forgive*, she believed, *otherwise we only hurt ourselves with endless bitterness*.

Anna chortled, "Eddie, you know there's no such thing as a new car since we entered the war. This here is a 1940 model. It's sturdy and good on fuel."

"I imagine Frank helped get it for you," Eddie blurted. "How did you get enough ration coupons to buy fuel for a joy ride up here and back to Marquette?" Eddie asked with a twinkle in his eye.

"Now, Eddie, quit badgering Anna. These days you must use your ingenuity, right, Anna? And we are so happy to see you both," Mary said, smiling as she passed around venison, gravy, potatoes, and homemade bread, encouraging everyone to eat.

"Frank and I saved up gas coupons," Anna answered. "Anyway, this is a special occasion," she continued sarcastically. "Ruth wanted to visit, and she just told me that she joined the Army, so it will be her last chance to look around our old stomping grounds before she ships out to God knows where."

"My goodness," Mary exclaimed, "how brave of you!"

"Good for you," Eddie said, but Ruth felt his embarrassment. She knew he desperately wanted to serve in the war, but the draft board refused him, claiming he had flat feet. Ruth found this ridiculous since Eddie hiked and hunted all over the hills and woods for many miles around Big Bay. How could he do that with flat feet? She suspected one of his rich employers pulled strings to keep him home and looking after their properties.

"When are you leaving?" Mary asked Ruth, passing more food around the table.

"After Christmas," Ruth answered, feeling relieved she would spend the holiday in the States.

"Do you know where you'll go?" Eddie asked. "We will have to track you."

"Track me? What do you mean?" Ruth asked puzzled.

"On our world map. See over on that large wall back in that corner behind the fireplace? Mary and I keep up with all the major campaigns and the whereabouts of people we know if we can. You'll have a pin, just like Joe. Did you know he's in the Pacific somewhere? I guess he'll miss the action in Europe."

"Joe?" Anna said, "You mean Ruthie's old boyfriend? You don't still have a crush on that Ojibwe boy, do you?" She taunted Ruth like a bully.

Mary interjected, asking Ruth, "You and Eddie and Joe were all friends when you were little kids, right?"

"And Jack," Ruth answered, feeling angry at Anna. "We had a lot of fun back then running around Big Bay. We all felt sad when they took Joe away from his mother after his father died in that logging accident. She was kind to us kids, and she made beautiful baskets."

"What happened to her, I wonder?" Mary said.

"She died soon after they took him away. I guess she felt she had nothing to live for after she lost her husband and son," Eddie said. "It was rotten of them to send him to that Indian School in Mount Pleasant. They killed her."

"Oh come, Eddie, you're telling stories. She drank herself to death," Anna laughed.

"She never drank before. She took to the drink after they took her son away," Eddie retorted.

"She drank to deaden the pain and it killed her," Ruth added.

"Joe told me hatred consumed him after his mother died," Eddie continued. "They didn't even tell him. Once he found out, he ran away from that cursed school. I don't know how he managed it, but he made his way on foot to the Straits, got across the water somehow to the Upper Peninsula, then walked to Bay Mills to find his father's family. He told me the journey cleared his head."

"That's over two hundred miles," Ruth said.

Anna yawned, bored. Ruth hated how ugly she looked when her nastiness bloomed.

Eddie continued, "Yes, over two hundred miles. When he found his father's family, they helped him get into the Marquette CCC camp over in Chippewa County. You know, the one with the best baseball team. Most of those campers were older, prominent Ojibwe men with skills in woodworking and other crafts. I think they helped Joe recover from his grief. When I saw him shortly before he enlisted in the Army, he seemed different. Calm. Stronger."

Still stewing over Anna's comment, Ruth recalled how Joe comforted her when she overheard someone at church say she was not as pretty as her sisters. *Don't worry about those old bats. They don't know nothing*, Joe had said, imitating a bat with his arms and making her laugh through her tears as they sat on a bleached-out log washed up on the shoreline. *I think you're pretty. You're better than the whole lot of them*, he reassured her, giving her a quick kiss on her cheek—her first kiss. The memory of that innocent kiss always made Ruth smile.

"Do you know where he is now?" she asked.

"No, just somewhere in the Pacific. We get letters from him with a San Francisco postmark. Funny how Joe just showed up here that day," Eddie said. "I looked up and there he was. I never heard a thing. He sure is good in the woods—the best. He taught me everything I know. Sometimes we walked through the woods for hours without even saying a word. Not everyone understands silence."

"I wonder how they've been treating him in the Army," Ruth said. "People can be so cruel. I know he ran into rough times here. But you would think no one has time for that during wartime."

"You know, based on my experience with my fellow man, there are always plenty who make time for cruelty," Eddie responded. "Say, that reminds me. We got a new book by Somerset Maugham we wanted to give you. It's called *The Razor's Edge*. A slim volume you can stash in your trunk. A bit like *Lost Horizon*. Deep. Spiritual. But common sense, too."

"I voted for a light romance, but you know Eddie. He thinks too much, and thinks everyone else should, too," Mary laughed, bending toward him to put her arm through his.

"You haven't read it yet, have you?" Eddie asked, adding, "I know you read a lot."

Ruth would have said no, even if she had, but in this case she had not and having a hardcover book would be a treasure. "No, I haven't read it yet." Ruth got up and gave Eddie and Mary each a long hug. "Thank you, both."

CHAPTER 3

DARK PASSAGE

(APRIL 1945)

Ruth stood on the upper deck of the S.S. *Lurline*, mesmerized by the final loading of the ship for its return trip across the Pacific Ocean. With its luxurious interior striped away and its brilliant white hull camouflaged in dull gray paint, the liner that once sailed the Hawaii tourist route now zigzagged across the Pacific avoiding Japanese submarines to ferry troops and equipment in the fight against Imperial Japan.

Having boarded hours earlier with her hospital unit, Ruth, now Second Lieutenant Amundsen, wiggled into a spot on the over-packed deck, squeezing between her fellow Army nurses to watch the final boarding below. A wave of giddiness filled her as she breathed in the smells of salt, diesel, and canvas. She felt awed by the size and beauty of the ship.

A din rose from the stream of Army men below, dressed in new, green field uniforms as they shuffled onto the ship. Ruth marveled at the steady bob of helmets and bedrolls secured over the tops and sides of each backpack, rifles shouldered, and duffle bags perched on each right shoulder. The rhythm of competing chants and singsongs filled the air. Sergeants yelled "stay in line!" and "fill the gap!" and "keep moving!" They received the ritualized reply, "Yes, Sergeant!"

Ruth saw the line moved as fast as possible as each GI inched forward, pressing against a backpack to his front, but after three months of training she understood yelling served a purpose in Army life. It focused soldiers' minds on something they could fear or hate more than the impending ocean voyage or the Japanese enemy—their sergeant. Yelling also fought off the slow-motion boredom of loading four thousand soldiers onto the ship.

The sun beat on Ruth's face, forcing her to hold a hand up to shield her eyes. Ruth felt the tightness of every crammed space on the ship, but more and more troops kept filing on board. She could not see an end to the trucks and buses queued to unload each unit.

"How much longer is this loading going to take!" Alice Silva exclaimed. "It seems like we've been here days already. We had plenty of time to go into San Francisco on pass if they'd let us."

One of Ruth's seven bunk mates, Alice, graduated from nursing school in Sacramento the previous fall. She stood a head taller than Ruth. Her dark, wavy hair, which she secured into a tight bun when in uniform, fell below her shoulders. Alice's perfectly proportioned face reminded Ruth of a classical sculpture. She came from a small town of Portuguese immigrants in central California and like Ruth, she joined the Army hoping for some excitement, travel, and a steady income. At first her parents, first generation immigrants, tried to stop her. They feared her beauty would attract dangerous attention, but Alice argued that she could handle whatever came her way and lacking any brothers, she felt an obligation to serve. Ruth mused on their first meeting.

"Did they give you their blessing?" Ruth had asked when they met at Letterman General Hospital a few days earlier, when Alice and a few other West Coast nurses joined their hospital unit.

"Not exactly, but they didn't stop me, so here I am," Alice laughed.

Although four years older, Ruth felt a kinship with Alice after a senior nurse questioned her sense of patriotism and Alice replied, "Patriotism? I'm as patriotic as anyone else, but you can't eat patriotism, can you, ma'am?"

Alice broke into Ruth's thoughts to ask, "Where do you think we will end up over there?" as she pointed west toward the Pacific. "I hope it's Hawaii. Wouldn't that be great?"

"Hawaii would be wonderful," Ruth said thinking of the palm trees and the tropical fruit she wanted to taste.

"Lieutenants," First Lieutenant Esther Wilson, the head nurse, interrupted as she appeared behind them without warning—a habit she seemed to have mastered. "We won't hide out in the rear in the Territory of Hawaii or Australia anymore. We'll get closer to the action, I'm sure."

Although only one rank senior to them, Wilson might as well have been a General. Many younger nurses dodged her as they caught sight of her curly, red hair flashing like a warning beacon. With a demeanor that mixed grimness with determined optimism, Wilson impressed Ruth since she first met her in Kansas when their hospital unit formed, and they trained to go overseas.

Ruth recalled how moved she felt when Wilson talked about her experiences nursing in the tunnels of Corregidor in the Philippines during the Japanese bombardment before General MacArthur retreated. Answering a question about how nurses worked in the pitch-black tunnels when the Japanese bombardment repeatedly knocked out the generators and dirt fell on the patients, Wilson told them, "You never know what hidden strengths and ingenuity you have until you need them. None of us ever dreamed Manila would be attacked. We were soft from light duty and dinner parties, but when the Japanese invaded, I am proud to say everyone found the courage and determination to keep going. Sometimes that's all you need to do—keep going from one day to the next. I know each of you will, too."

Hearing Wilson talk, Ruth felt admiration for her courage and compassion. She did not know if she could match it. *I'll do my best*, she thought.

Ruth considered Wilson lucky to be among the Army nurses who had escaped the Japanese in 1942, but once over too many shots of whiskey at a party, Wilson leaned toward Ruth bleary eyed. Crying, she had suddenly grabbed Ruth's arm saying, "I should have been with them." Even after the liberation and safe return of the seventy-seven nurses captured on the Bataan Peninsula earlier that year, Wilson did not seem relieved of her sense of guilt. Ruth believed Wilson hoped to return to the Philippines as a kind of penance.

Now, Wilson barked, "Don't expect a soft assignment like Hawaii. We've liberated the Philippines and our troops are moving up toward the Japanese islands. We'll go where we're needed and for as long as we are needed."

Ruth and Alice exchanged a look. Ruth understood Wilson already knew their destination and had given them a clue—either the islands of Japan or the Philippines, so no Hawaii. After Wilson moved down the line to talk to other nurses standing along the railing, Ruth and Alice began to speculate.

Alice whispered to Ruth, "I heard some infantry officers at chow this morning. They claimed the 'mop up' operations MacArthur crowed about back in February killed many of our soldiers and civilians, too. It's some of the worst fighting yet and still going on around Manila."

"I heard the same thing," Ruth said. "I hope we don't go there."

Rumors about the Philippines contradicted the news-papers. Back in October when Ruth volunteered, General MacArthur gave his "I have returned" speech on Leyte Island, which created excitement throughout the U.S., but the war in the Pacific went on. After Ruth left Wisconsin for medical training near Chicago in early February, MacAr-thur declared Manila liberated. She began to wonder if the Pacific War would end soon. Many people at home believed the Pearl of the Orient, Manila, had been saved. But the Army grapevine told a different, darker story of destruction and excessive casualties. Ruth heard men curse General MacAr-thur for wasting his soldiers fighting over one pile of rubble after another as the Japanese fought to the death in Manila.

"We just have to wait and see. Let's get across this ocean first," Ruth eventually concluded, and Alice nodded in agreement.

As they watched the soldiers coming aboard, some of them looked up and saw the group of nurses in their dress uniforms. They waved and whistled until a sergeant hit a few of them in the head. "Keep your eyes down here, soldier, or you will trip up the whole line."

Ruth and Alice laughed, but Wilson rushed up to them, and said, "Ladies, don't encourage them."

"Ah, come on, Lieutenant Wilson, let them have a little fun. How many of them do you think will even make it back home, huh?" Alice said.

"General quarters, general quarters! All hands on deck!" blared over a loudspeaker near where the nurses stood.

"What on earth is that?" Alice cried.

"Testing," Wilson said, "But you will hear that a lot on this trip if they spot Japanese subs and planes." She paused before continuing. "This is going to take at least a couple more hours before the ship sets sail. I suggest you ladies get your quarters sorted and check the duty roster, so you know what shift you are working. I will let you know when we're getting ready to cast off. You don't want to miss that or going under the Golden Gate Bridge."

As Ruth walked back to her cabin with Alice, she imagined the rich luxury of the ship from the details of brass and covered wood floors that peeked out on the bridge and in the captain's quarters, which she, Alice, and other nurses had toured soon after they boarded several hours before. The captain seemed to enjoy having young nurses onboard, and they jumped at the chance when he invited them to see the bridge and his quarters.

Stuffing away the few things they brought into the crowded cabin, Ruth marveled at her experiences of the previous three months. If she had remained in the Upper Peninsula for an entire lifetime, she would never have seen or done any of the things she'd recently experienced.

She said to Alice, "I can't believe I started this year orienteering in the snow in Wisconsin."

"You mean Fort McCoy? Isn't that a prisoner-of-war camp? I heard they held that Japanese prisoner from Pearl Harbor," Alice said.

"It does have a POW camp. We didn't see much of that. I heard they also hold Germans and Italians. We stayed in the training area. A lot of people from the Midwest start there when they join. I found orienteering in the snow a waste of time, but we did learn how to dress and act like soldiers, I guess. I was glad to move on to Chicago. I learned a bit about burn care and plastic surgery, but I hated working in the psych ward."

"Oh me, too. I worked in one in Sacramento. I didn't like the padded cells and the straitjackets. And the screaming of grown men unsettled me. Some of them were so violent. I couldn't take it," Alice said.

When they heard a horn blast, someone yelled, "They're getting ready to cast off. Come now if you want to see the ship leave."

Ruth had developed a deep reverence for Lake Superior and the natural wealth of the Upper Peninsula's lakes and trees. But as the ship sailed under the Golden Gate Bridge and left San Francisco Bay for the open ocean, she began to see an expanded natural grandeur on the ocean. It was one thing to read about the ocean, but to experience the taste of salt and the wind whipping across the deep blue water exhilarated Ruth.

The first week of the voyage West sorted out who would enjoy the trip and who would not. Ruth felt giddy excitement to be going out to sea on such a huge ship. She forgot her terror about what she would do if she were ever thrown into the water not knowing how to swim.

The captain had advised everyone to get up for breakfast and fresh air each morning, even when it stormed. Ruth followed his advice, rising early and walking as much as possible. *It's better than swaying in a hammock all day like*

Mabel, Ruth thought. Mabel refused to leave her hammock the first week. She persuaded her cabin mates to cover for her on hospital shifts and bring her meals until Lieutenant Wilson found out and ordered her to get up.

"None of my nurses are going to act like that sickly bunch of GIs we treat in sick bay each day," Wilson said.

Clusters of seasick personnel had spread throughout the ship, nausea hitting some of the men especially hard while living in their smelly cabins crammed with twelve to fourteen men. At night with the portholes shut tight in blackout conditions, the men complained that the smell of dirty socks did not help settle their stomachs in the rolling seas.

While Ruth loved the mornings on the ocean, she never tired of the nightly show of unfamiliar stars. One evening as she stood outside her cabin watching the stars during blackout, she felt the presence of someone standing next to her.

"Evening, ma'am," he whispered, barely audible over the sound of the sea.

Ruth felt frightened. She had heard stories of the women on board being accosted and worried she'd made a mistake coming out. But something kind in the man's voice made her linger instead of fleeing back to her cabin.

Ruth nodded, although she knew he could not see her, and she only saw a shadow of him. "Good evening," she answered quietly.

She met him again on deck the next morning, smoking a cigarette: something forbidden to do outside at night in case a Japanese sub picked up the light. An older man, he looked soft around the waistline with a receding hairline and pudgy, pink face. Ruth wondered how he handled all the work on deck at his age.

"Did you stand here last night?" Ruth asked.

"Yes, this is my favorite spot for breaks," he said. "I come up here from the galley to get fresh air. I'm normally a steward, but I help out where I'm needed these days. It's hot as the dickens down there."

"You like to hang out near the nurses' quarters?" Ruth felt suspicious, wondering if he was a pervert after all.

"Oh no, nothing like that." he said flicking his finished cigarette overboard before lighting a second one, "I'm a happily married man with three girls. See." He pulled out a family picture he kept in his wallet. The worn picture showed three girls with long black hair sitting in front of him with a younger Asian woman, also with long hair, who Ruth suspected might be his wife. "That's the way they looked four years ago when this thing started. They don't look like that now, but I like this picture. I like to hear girls talking and giggling. It settles me somehow."

"Is that your wife?" Ruth asked.

"We met in Honolulu. We've been married over ten years now," he said studying Ruth's face as if assessing her reaction. "She's Hawaiian and Chinese," he added. "You'll find a lot of Asians and mixed races on the islands."

"She's beautiful. So are your girls," Ruth said, feeling embarrassed she could not tell the difference between them and the Japanese.

"That's the wife's doing. God knows they didn't get their looks from me," he laughed.

"Have you been on the *Lurline* long?" Ruth asked.

"I'm a regular member of the crew. Even before the war, I went back and forth between Honolulu and San Francisco. That's how I met my wife. Those were grand trips. I hope we do them again after the war. I was on the ship when they attacked Pearl Harbor. That was tense."

"What happened?" Ruth asked, feeling frightened and angry at the mention of Pearl Harbor.

"We were two days out of Honolulu with about eight hundred people on board, more than usual, because we had the tourists and military families evacuating Hawaii. Something was in the air, but we had no idea the Japanese would attack. We came near another cargo vessel that a sub threatened, but we didn't see anything. We went into blackout—painting and covering all the windows—and headed out as fast as we could, zigzagging all the way to San Francisco Bay."

"Sounds terrifying," Ruth said, wondering if they would be attacked on this trip.

"The worst part was not knowing if my wife and kids were safe. On board was fine. When you're doing your job, you don't think about fear, you know? You just keep working. It all worked out fine though; my family was safe. That was all that mattered to me," he said.

He laughed, lightening the mood. "The best part about it was the passengers became very cooperative. You know the type, the ones with money who love to complain and demand? Anyway, they stayed quiet as church mice and never left their cabins all the way back. No skeet shooting. No dress up dancing. Just a quiet run. Jackie Robinson was on that trip. He played poker all the way back to port."

"Do you think we'll make it this time?" Ruth asked, feeling anxious.

"Oh, sure. I think our boys have the Japanese on the run now. Anyway, we go as fast as we can, zigzagging so it's harder to track us. We've lost some cargo ships, but the *Lurline* is a lucky ship. Don't you worry, ma'am. We'll be just fine."

Trying to add something to distract Ruth from the possibility of the ship sinking, he said, "You know, before the war, we took Amelia Earhart and her plane across to Honolulu for her solo return flight. She was something. A real beauty and down-to-earth. Her plane was a beauty, too."

"I've met her," Ruth said, excited to share her meeting with the famed pilot. "I shook her hand when she visited my high school in Marquette, Michigan in the 1930s. I'll never forget what she told us: something like, *The most difficult thing is the decision to act. The rest is tenacity. The fears are paper tigers. You can do anything you decide to do.* She was just great and inspired us all."

"Is Amelia Earhart why you joined the Army?" he asked.

Ruth laughed, "I haven't thought of her in years. She was larger than life." *I'm just ordinary*, Ruth thought, but added, "You know, maybe she did influence me, like you said. She made me want to do something special with my life."

"Seems plain enough to me, especially since you met her. Listen, I'm sorry if I shook you up earlier, but let me give you a tip. If we do run into trouble, make your way to one of these lifeboats. You see the ones lashed to the side of the ship? We don't have enough for everyone, but you might have a chance if you can get there."

"Oh, thanks," Ruth replied, wondering how she would do that.

"And keep wearing your life jacket when you walk around just like you are now. Once we get further out, you might have to sleep in it, too," he said, flicking his cigarette into the wind, which carried it out to sea.

CHAPTER 4

PEARL OF THE ORIENT

(MAY 1945)

———

Ruth opened the Matson Line's *Wireless* newsletter from May 8th, that she kept folded as a keepsake, declaring "V-E DAY!" in thick block letters across a third of the front page. As she sat out of the wind, relishing the golden rays of sunrise spreading across the Pacific Ocean, Ruth felt her stomach lurch. She tried to relax into the power of the ocean. The ocean breeze refreshed her after the stuffiness of the cabin, but she felt uneasy. *Will people forget about us out here in the Pacific now that war is over in Europe?* Ruth wondered.

Alice walked quickly and carefully toward her, having mastered how to walk on the rolling ship, her life vest securely fastened. She sat next to Ruth.

"There you are. Did you hear the news? They exchanged movies last night with that cargo ship when they transferred that appendix case, so they can show different movies.

Tonight, is the *Purple Heart* starring Dana Andrews. It's about the Pacific war."

"Did that guy make it?" Ruth asked. Not waiting for an answer, she said, "I've never seen anything like that basket swinging in the air between the two ships. It seemed like he'd fall into the ocean every time the two ships moved apart. I thought the line would snap for sure."

"It did look dangerous, but one of the crew told me later the ship captain does this all the time, so he knows what he's doing. Anyway, the guy made it through surgery and he's recovering. You might see him on your next shift. I hear Colonel Bateman did a good job stitching him up. According to him, you know, he's the most prominent plastic surgeon in Chicago," Alice laughed. "Funny. That merchant marine could never afford a fancy doctor like that back in the States. But here in the middle of the Pacific Ocean, just by chance, he not only has his appendix removed for free, but he gets stitched back together by Chicago's best plastic surgeon."

"I don't like the Colonel. He's loud and arrogant and I don't like how he comes on to the nurses. The man has a wife and children at home for goodness sake," Ruth said.

"He's a brilliant surgeon, but a heel. He tried it with me a few nights ago when I was alone with him on shift. He cornered me, offering a drink from that silver flask he carries around," Alice said. "He really scared me because of his rank, but I broke away. The worst thing is, I guess someone saw us, and word got back to Wilson, so she yelled at me yesterday for chasing after a married man and senior officer. Why do I always get blamed for men attacking me?"

Ruth sighed in sympathy. "Wilson should know better." Before she met Alice, Ruth assumed beautiful women had it made, but Alice taught her about the ugliness she sometimes faced. Ruth noticed Alice never wore lipstick or nail polish or fixed her hair like everyone else, but it made no difference. All the men ogled her, and some women seemed to hate her.

Changing the subject back to *Purple Heart*, Ruth said, "I saw that movie last year when it came out. I can't watch the Japanese torture our men again. I'd rather do something else. Maybe I'll write a letter and listen to the big-band music hour tonight, instead."

"I've seen it too, but it's something to do. I think the Army believes these movies prepare us for what lies ahead. They sure make the men mad as hell. Do you suppose the Japanese are as brutal as everyone says? What will they do to us if they have the chance?" Alice asked.

Ruth shrugged her shoulders, feeling helpless. "I guess we'll just deal with whatever happens, like Wilson always says." She tried to sound lighthearted. To herself she prayed they would never face Japanese torture. She wasn't sure she could handle it. She felt so weak inside when she thought about it.

When they crossed the International Dateline several days earlier, they learned they were headed to Manila. Ruth reread the paragraphs in the newsletter about the ongoing fighting in the Philippines, which Alice now took from her to read aloud.

"It says here the Japanese don't care the Germans surrendered. They'll fight on. Oh, and here's another report of a Japanese suicide. I don't get that." Looking up from the paper, Alice said, "Some of the crew let it slip that a kamikaze pilot flew into the USS *Comfort* after we left San Francisco, killing nurses and doctors, but I've never seen a report of it in the newsletter and no one has said anything officially. I wonder if it's true?"

"I don't know, but the crew seems to know a lot more about what's going on in this ocean than we do," Ruth said.

"No one will be safe from the Japanese anywhere if they all commit suicide to kill us," Alice sighed. "Let's get some chow before it gets too crowded. I'm starved."

Ruth nodded, following her lead after she took the paper and refolded it back into the book her cousin Eddie gave her before she left for training. She held it tight in the bend of her arm to secure the papers inside, including Margaret's letter about her flight nurse training. The book cover had torn off, leaving a slender black volume with gold letters that looked worn from handling. She had read *The Razor's Edge* twice so far on the voyage, and now it also served as a kind of diary. *Eddie was right to give me this*, Ruth realized. The story prodded her to think about her life after war if she made it through.

With her unit nurses, Ruth had settled into a comfortable routine of rotating hospital shifts, continuous training, movies, reading, card games, and listening to music broadcast over the ship's loudspeaker. Her bunkmates often took over the cabin for games of rummy while they chain-smoked cigarettes, usually driving Ruth outside to walk in the fresh air. *Everyone seems to smoke except me*, Ruth thought each time she vainly waved a cloud of smoke out of her face.

When she escaped her cabin to walk around, Ruth always saw soldiers leaning against duffle bags or bulkheads, studying pocket-sized Armed Services Edition books. Ruth had never seen so many regular guys reading, and though she preferred hardcover books, the plentiful paperbound books expanded her reading options. The ship librarian told her the soldiers preferred books by American authors—like Jack London, F. Scott Fitzgerald, John Dos Passos, and Ernest

Hemingway—that the Germans banned and burned. Ruth smiled thinking, *This mass-reading is a kind of democratic defiance against Hitler.*

After breakfast as Ruth walked by one soldier, leaning up against a wall reading *The Grapes of Wrath,* she wondered how Anna found Oklahoma and if her sister would be able to send care packages as she'd promised, excited by the idea of getting a package from home. *I must write her, but what can I say?* Ruth worried. *Everything seems to be classified secret.*

As they got closer to Manila, Lieutenant Wilson gave them pep talks about what to expect, although she had not been to the Philippines since 1942. "Manila is the most beautiful city I ever saw," she said one day as she became animated reminiscing about her pre-war days. "Wide boulevards lined with trees, grand buildings in classical style: they call it the Pearl of the Orient. I loved taking the trolley around the city or riding in a horse-drawn cart. The palm trees are everywhere. And so many different types of flowers. It's a huge city. I know they've had a tough time, but it can't have changed that much."

Ruth hoped Lieutenant Wilson would be right. But the boys she met in San Francisco returning from the campaign told of wanton destruction by the Japanese forces seeking revenge, and American forces using artillery and bombs to ferret out or destroy the remaining Japanese hidden in buildings throughout the city.

A few days later, Ruth and Alice stood next to Lieutenant Wilson and the other nurses as the *Lurline* entered Manila Harbor. They huddled together waiting to disembark. The captain threaded the ship through a well-marked lane between the remaining wreckage of ships and planes. As the ship slowed down to dock, the breeze off the ocean stopped, replaced by a smelly, damp heat that sickened Ruth as she struggled to get a breath of fresh air. She felt her face and back dripping in sweat. She took a quick sip from her canteen, but the tepid water brought no relief.

Softly, Wilson cried, "Oh my god, the city is gone. It's all gone. How can it all be gone?"

Alice and Ruth turned to follow Wilson's gaze over columns of Army trucks maneuvering through the ruined landscape. A few buildings stood partially-destroyed and a few seemed unharmed, but there was no city, no palms trees—nothing but a ragged landscape.

"It's gone," Wilson repeated. Ruth saw shock on Wilson's face, but she quickly regained her composure and began directing the women.

The relief Ruth felt to be getting off the ship onto solid land and getting down to work was replaced by the shock that they would exit the ship down the cargo nets, which meant swaying over the water and carefully going backward down the ropes, hand over hand. Ruth prayed her arms would not give out or her shoes would not slip off on the ropes. Her bag, strapped across her body, suddenly felt heavier. Wilson had anticipated the cargo net and made sure the nurses wore their new, khaki work uniforms, converted from male-issued pants and shirts. She knew the men often caught a look up the skirts of the women, and she made sure to prepare her nurses.

Once Ruth reached solid ground, she felt relieved to make it safely but was unsteady after weeks of swaying on the ship. The urgency of the need for more medical support put them at the front of the line, but they waited impatiently by the dock for trucks to take to them where they would set up their hospital unit in Manila. The heat and humidity felt suffocating.

Ruth struggled to pull herself up into the high truck, her arms and legs weakened by the climb down the cargo net. As they drove through the city in open trucks, Ruth's stomach lurched at each bump. The air smelled like a haze of oil and smoke, mixed with something else. She felt overwhelmed. "What's that smell?" someone asked. "It smells awful."

"Rotting bodies—people and animals," someone else answered. "I'd recognize that smell anywhere. It's something you can never forget."

"Oh, that's nothing." Ruth heard a sergeant yell, as he rode with them at the back of the truck. "A couple months ago the dust and the smell could kill you." He laughed. "It's much better now, but you can get use to anything," he said, sounding like a wise old man in a teenager's body.

Ruth stole a glance at Wilson, wondering what she thought of seeing no trace of the Pearl of the Orient at street level. Building-sized piles of debris lined the road, which was filled with a jumble of military vehicles maneuvering past them. It appeared that the roadway had been cleared of most of the debris, but it would take time to remove or rebuild what remained.

Ruth returned the smiles and waves to the Filipinos running alongside the truck, mostly women and children, some waving American flags. Many stood in front of makeshift shacks that partially concealed the wasteland behind them. Army photographers with the convoy captured their smiles of welcome.

"Come on, girls, how about a smile for the camera," a photographer in khaki uniform yelled, pointing at their truck filled with a fresh batch of nurses. Ruth smiled obediently with the other nurses, even though she felt on the verge of a breakdown from the scale of suffering she started to realize lay behind those happy smiles.

CHAPTER 5

NO END IN SIGHT

(JUNE – JULY 1945)

JUNE 1945 — MANILA

Ruth choked on the mix of dust, humidity, and heat as she lay under her mosquito net. She struggled to sleep, often waking from a dream of tall glasses filled with ice. She loved the work, but the tropical heat wore her down. Multiple waves of casualties funneled into the hospital, making each day feel like several crushed together. Ruth felt trapped in an endless loop of fitful sleep, tropical heat, and tasteless meals. Stolen naps and Army coffee kept her going.

When will I get used to this? Ruth asked herself.

The hospital compound—a mix of multiple medical units—sat near the port to facilitate evacuation of casualties. It took several days for a crew of Army logistics soldiers and Filipino workers to squeeze their general hospital in among the network of canvas tents and confiscated buildings. But that hardly mattered since Wilson put the nurses to work right away helping adjoining hospitals. Specialty wards expanded weekly as the Army put up more tents and found more usable buildings.

Before Manila, Ruth easily recalled patients' names and faces. But in the endless stream of casualties, Ruth remembered cases—compound fractures, gunshot wounds, tetanus, amputations, tropical diseases, gangrene, venereal disease—instead of individuals. The faces of the young men blurred together, as minor cases returned to duty and the rest left on evacuation ships and planes.

"That bastard got me good," a bayonet casualty from Arkansas remarked, retelling his story of near death fighting a Japanese soldier. "If the medic hadn't stuffed my intestines back in and wrapped me up, I'd a been a goner," he laughed. Ruth thought he would not make it when he first arrived. Now safely out of danger after surgery as he waited for evacuation, he joked about the length of his scar and embellished his story.

Overhearing him one day, Lieutenant Wilson said to Ruth, "By the time he gets home, General Yamashita himself will have been the one who tried to kill him."

Ruth laughed at hearing the name of the commander of the Japanese army still fighting up in the mountains, realizing the Army and the war had twisted her sense of humor into something neither Anna nor Linda would recognize.

Ruth left the ward for a break to huddle with Alice and other nurses enjoying a brief smoke break on packing crates. Ruth did not smoke, but she often joined the smokers for the companionship.

"This heat is awful," Alice cried, wiping her face with a man's handkerchief held in her right hand while she took a long drag from the cigarette in her left.

"How you can smoke in this heat? The humidity drains the life out of me," Ruth said dabbing her sleeve to her brow. "I can't stop sweating."

"Smoking distracts me and covers the smells of I-don't-know-what," replied Alice with a laugh.

"You'll get used to it," a nurse from Louisiana said, looking fresh and cool, as she took short puffs from her cigarette. "Drink more water and make sure you take your salt tablets."

"Sweating is good," Alice said. "It's when you stop that you have to worry about heatstroke, unless you're like Louisiana here who thrives in this weather. I never see you sweat." Alice laughed.

"In another month, you'll be the same. You won't even notice the heat." Louisiana smiled as she took a final drag before tossing the butt onto the littered ground.

Lieutenant Wilson walked quickly up to them and said, "I need someone to help a doctor with a burn case. Amundsen, why don't you go; it will take your mind off the weather." Wilson spoke with a grim smile.

"I don't have a lot of experience with burns," Ruth answered, feeling uncertain she knew what to do.

"He'll tell you what to do. Just go. Hurry," she said, pointing to the tent.

Ruth walked out of the bright sunlight into the shaded tent. It took a moment for her eyes to adjust but she followed a man's voice yelling, "Over here, Lieutenant, help me turn him."

Ruth studied the soldier, who was burned halfway up his body like he had been dipped into a fire. The smell of the singed flesh nauseated her. Ruth heard him moaning in pain and wondered if the doctor was treating him for shock.

"Put your hands here," he said pointing to the man's left side and thigh. "Help me turn him over. Careful. I don't know how he'll hold together."

As Ruth put her hands gently on the soldier, she began to turn him over. Ruth's eyes widened when the patient's leg separated from the rest of the body at the knee.

"Don't worry about that. The fire severed the cartilage and tissue there," the doctor said, studying her. "It happens. Hey, you're not going to faint on me, are you, Lieutenant?" He sounded like he hoped she would.

Ruth felt anger rising. *You might have told me, you bastard*, she thought. Out loud she said, "You knew his leg had separated? Did you think it would be funny?" Ruth gave him a look of disgust. "You're a doctor, for God's sake, not a circus clown."

The doctor looked like Ruth had slapped him. "Sorry, I didn't mean anything by it. I've seen too much that I can't do anything about. I forgot myself. Please help me turn him. I really do need to look at his back for a bullet. And I need your help bandaging him."

After they finished wrapping him, and the patient slept with the help of morphine, the doctor said to Ruth, "Look, I'm sorry about that little joke. We tend to initiate the new nurses. I know it was in bad taste, but you passed, by the way," he said smiling. "You're cool under pressure."

"Did Wilson put you up to this?" Ruth asked, suspicious that Wilson had made Ruth the brunt of a bad joke.

He shook his head. "She didn't know anything about it. Please don't tell her. She'll never help me again."

"Don't worry. She'll always help a patient, doctor," Ruth responded. She felt angry and embarrassed, even though, as he said, she had passed the test. It made her mad that anyone would make a joke at a patient's expense. *That poor man will be a cripple for the rest of his life*, Ruth thought.

After Ruth told Wilson and the nurses about the incident, everyone became more cautious in dealing with the doctors, especially the ones they did not know. In their unit Colonel Bateman seemed to be their main problem, and Wilson warned the nurses about his roaming hands. More importantly, Wilson cautioned the nurses to guard the medicine cabinet with their lives. "Don't let patients, even doctors, get into the cabinet. No matter what. If you have a problem, call me."

JULY 1945 — BATANGAS

In early July, Ruth's unit received orders to move south to Batangas to co-locate with other hospitals at a growing logistics base near the port in order to accelerate evacuations of casualties back to Hawaii and the States. Ruth thought the move out of Manila would bring relief from the sight of ruins and desperate women and children wandering the streets. She also hoped for fresher air outside the city.

"It's just like Manila," Alice said as they sat next to each other in the back of the Army truck with side seats pulled down for the nurses to sit on. "So much destruction." She spoke as they passed flattened buildings along the road.

When they stopped for a rest at Lipa, the chaplain gathered them together for a moment of silence for the eleven American prisoners of war tortured and murdered there in November 1944. Ruth felt guilty those men had been suffering here when she and Anna visited Eddie and Mary, oblivious to their nightmare. It made her feel responsible somehow. The stories of the Japanese Army's attacks on civilians followed a familiar script: rape; torture; murder; the routine bayoneting of men, women, and children, even babies. The atrocities in Batangas also included blowing up buildings packed with civilians and stuffing victims down wells.

It will take months, even years, Ruth thought, *to find all the dead.*

Ruth suspected the jungle would conceal many victims forever, as if they had never existed. She hoped Japanese prisoners of war would do the work of recovering the dead in Batangas, even if American soldiers had to protect them from angry Filipinos as they had in Manila. The wantonness of the killing spree disgusted Ruth.

"Dehumanization," Wilson said, as if reading Ruth's mind as they sat next to each other in the back of the truck after they left Lipa.

"What?" Ruth asked.

"The Japanese believe they are the master race, just like the Nazis, so the rest of us, including the Filipinos, are less than human. Therefore, they kill and torture without remorse. Dehumanization."

"That can't be true," Ruth said startled. "They're not evil."

"Don't be so sure. War can make anyone commit evil."

As the convoy pulled off the road and came to a stop, all Ruth could see was a small muddy clearing surrounded by dense jungle. Someone asked, "Where's the logistics base?"

"This is it. We're opening up this area on the north side of the compound," Colonel Bateman answered, waving at the jungle as he walked back from his jeep at the head of the convoy. "Let's get moving."

Getting in and out of the Army trucks, which towered above her, always made Ruth nervous. Taller people, like Alice, easily climbed up into the back of the truck, while Ruth struggled to reach a metal foothold to push herself up and grabbed for the side of the truck. Dismounting required jumping to the ground, which scared Ruth, or finding the foothold again to help her get down. Now the last one to leave the truck, she decided to jump and stepped to the edge—hoping for the best—when the vehicle lurched forward, throwing Ruth off the back. She fell hard on her right kneecap, her head grazing the edge of the tailgate on the way down.

Ruth woke up looking into the eyes of a doctor and nurse she did not recognize.

"You're awake, Lieutenant. I'm Major Walters and this is Lieutenant Albright. How are you feeling?" he asked, and Ruth nodded in response, feeling groggy.

"Did you give me morphine?" Ruth asked, feeling disconnected from her body.

"A little. One of the hazards of being in a medical unit. The medic saw you were in a good deal of pain and he had a vial, so he gave it to you. I don't think you need anymore," the doctor answered.

"You took quite a fall off that truck," the doctor continued. "I can't tell you how often this happens. You bumped your head. No concussion, though. Anyway, we don't think the kneecap is fractured, but you have significant soft tissue damage, and you need to stay here for a while, then we'll shift you over to your quarters for recuperation. If we were back home, I would put you on bed rest for a month to make sure you healed, but seeing we're at war, I can give you a week after we release you."

"Where am I? Where's my unit?" Ruth asked, feeling lost in the absence of the familiar faces of her hospital unit.

"They're on the other side of the compound where your unit is clearing jungle to set up your hospital. Our unit got here a few weeks ago," the nurse answered. "Count yourself lucky you'll miss setting up operations in this heat." She smiled.

When Ruth moved into her quarters, they carried her on a stretcher. Crutches lay beside her cot. The nurses in her tent had set up Ruth's area next to Alice, so all Ruth had to do was lie down and sleep elevating her leg. Ruth smiled upon seeing Alice, who said, "Ruth, this sure is a primitive place. We're lucky they put down a rough cement floor for us or we'd still be on dirt with the snakes. How are you feeling?"

"I'm ready to get to work," Ruth responded, worrying about how to do her rounds with crutches.

"You won't be going to the wards yet. You need rest. Enjoy it. That doctor—wow, he's quite handsome, by the way, and single, too, they say. Anyway, he said you need a full week of recuperation, so don't worry about a thing. The Filipino girls will take care of you, getting your food and helping you back and forth from the latrine. We have it made. They do everything from wash our clothes, shine our shoes, even cook up some meals better than those C-rations or the mess hall. You settle back and rest. Here's your canteen for water," Alice said, tucking the container near Ruth's pillow and closing her mosquito net.

"Do you need anything else?" Alice asked, but Ruth drifted off to sleep before she could reply.

She woke up in the middle of the night to two pink eyes staring at her—a rat perched on the frame of her mosquito net, studying her. Sweat dripped down Ruth's face. "Get out of here," Ruth whispered, feeling too weak to raise a hand.

The rat did not move, seeming to assess Ruth's condition. Eventually, it jumped onto the ground and ran off into the dark.

After a few days Ruth returned to duty, arguing that she felt fine. Wilson assigned her to the night shift and paired her with Alice, who hovered over her.

"Ruth, sit down and write the charts. I'll pass out the meds. You came back to duty too soon. Your knee is not healed. Here, put your leg up on this chair. It should be elevated."

"Okay, Doc," Ruth laughed, submitting to her mothering. "I can help load syringes and prep meds if you move me closer to the medicine cabinet. How about it?"

It took a couple weeks before Ruth felt well enough to walk around. After months in the Philippines, Ruth thought she could withstand anything. That is, until some soldiers rushed in with a small boy who had been crushed by an Army truck as he ran alongside begging for food and had slipped. When the boy died on Ruth's shift, looking so tiny and helpless on the green Army cot covered in white sheeting, Wilson, making her rounds of the wards, took Ruth outside away from the hospital and let her sob until Ruth felt she could cry no more.

"Ruth, that boy is in a better place. You did everything possible. Here," Wilson said handing Ruth her canteen, "throw some water on your face, and let's go back to work. The boys are counting on us."

Soon after that accident, some Filipinos dressed in military uniforms brought a tall, skeletal man with patchy, blond hair and sunburned skin into Ruth's ward. Folded into a fetal position, he appeared too weak to stand or sit. Scars from beatings and torture covered his body. The doctor looked him over and decided the only thing they could do was to slowly give him nourishment to see if he could recover.

"We'll take a blood sample to figure out what all he has. Probably malaria. Maybe other diseases," the doctor told Wilson and Ruth as they discussed his care. "He's in rough shape. It will be a miracle if he recovers. He's been beaten without mercy for a long time."

They dubbed him "the Dutchman" because that's what the Filipino guerrillas who dropped him off called him. He could have been Dutch or Danish or Norwegian, or even German. Since he lacked any identification papers, and no one could communicate with him in English, Tagalog, or any European language they knew, he remained a mystery. They even tried sign language after doctors did not find anything physically preventing him from talking. The doctors concluded trauma caused his silence, as they had seen with some victims of shellshock.

One day while Ruth was on duty, an Army lieutenant came in looking for the Dutchman. "We believe he's a Nazi war criminal, or worse, a communist," he told Ruth. "I need to talk to him."

"Oh? What makes you think that?" Ruth asked as she studied his neatly-pressed uniform and shiny boots. He carried a notebook in one hand.

"That's classified," he answered.

"You know he doesn't talk, right?" Ruth said.

"We think he's faking it," he said raising his chin slightly, assuming an all-knowing look. Ruth thought, *He likely has no idea.*

Later, reporting to Wilson, Ruth said, "He wanted to arrest the Dutchman and take him away for interrogation, but I told the Lieutenant he was my patient and I couldn't release him without orders. I also told him he was in rough shape, maybe even contagious, so if he died, the Lieutenant would be responsible." Ruth laughed, adding, "I think I scared him when I said the Dutchman might be contagious. So, he left. He didn't say he'd be back."

"That's odd. He's probably just fishing around," Wilson said. "How is the Dutchman?"

"Better, but I think he'll take a long time to recover his strength. He's starting to keep food down, so I think we can move to solids in a few days," Ruth answered, thinking treatment of starvation was something she never expected to add to her skills.

Ruth found the Dutchman's presence comforting. He reminded her of stoic Scandinavians in the Upper Peninsula who had little to say even under the best circumstances. She sensed by the way he ate and nodded his head to indicate a thank you, that he must be educated. He acted like a gentleman. It made sense to Ruth that he had stopped talking. *He must have seen horrible things. I wonder if they killed his family in front of him*, Ruth thought.

Eventually, the Dutchman became a kind of mascot in the ward. The soldiers gave him whatever they did not want from their rations, saying, "Give it to the Dutchman." He ate everything, including the canned eggs with their disturbing green color.

In July they brought in a burned Japanese prisoner of war. None of the nurses wanted to care for him after their visit to Lipa, but Wilson ordered them to treat him like any other patient. Recalling how Wilson spoke of the inhumanity of the Japanese, Ruth grew angry. She confronted Wilson.

"How can you expect us to do this? You've seen what they did. Let him die for all I care," she snapped. "You said it yourself, they're inhuman. Anyway, the Black nurses are supposed to care for the POWs."

Wilson studied Ruth's face. "I did say that, but this man is our patient. This isn't about him: it's about us and our oath as nurses. You will treat him just as you would any casualty. It's your duty, and there aren't any Black medical units here yet. They're still up in Manila."

"He could slit our throats," Ruth yelled.

"He's in no condition to slit anyone's throat, and he'll have a guard. You will care for him. That's an order, Lieutenant," Wilson said, turning her back to Ruth and walking away—ending the discussion.

By late July, Ruth had toughened and, surprisingly, had even adjusted to the heat and humidity. Those few months had passed like years, but she loved every minute of it. She felt needed and confident. She'd even accepted the recovering Japanese POW, who now served as a ward boy, cleaning up around the hospital during the day and returning to the stockade each night.

The first time the Dutchman saw the Japanese ward boy, tears filled his eyes. The Japanese soldier also cried and had bowed almost to the ground. Ruth wondered about that scene. It seemed so strange that both men would cry.

"What do you think it meant?" Alice asked her when they discussed it at lunch.

"I don't know. Maybe the Dutchman cried thinking of what the Japanese did to him."

"Then, the Japanese soldier cried knowing what he did to other people? That doesn't sound right, though, after everything they've told us about them."

"I guess we'll never know," Ruth answered.

An endless stream of hospital ships came in and out of the Batangas port. Although most casualties survived thanks to a chain of medical care from frontline medics to aid stations to smaller hospitals to the general hospitals, the volume of casualties appalled Ruth, and the injuries they suffered made her believe many would struggle going forward.

CHAPTER 6

THE LONG WAY HOME

(AUGUST – DECEMBER 1945)

AUGUST 1945

Ruth listened to the reports of powerful bombs dropped on Hiroshima and Nagasaki in early August thinking, *Surely this will end the war*, but nothing changed.

"When will the war end?" Ruth overheard Alice asking Wilson, expecting her to know more than anyone else.

"I have no idea. They're still fighting in the mountains, and we're preparing to invade Japan. It doesn't look like it will end yet," Wilson answered.

While others grew restless, Ruth felt sad that her time in the Philippines might end soon. She missed Big Bay and talking with family, even sparring with her sister Linda, but she felt alive and confident in her work here.

As the days passed, Ruth became more aware of the Filipino world coming to life within and around their base. She loved their local fruits: especially mangoes, which she regularly bought from the women and children. She marveled at their ingenuity to take what seemed like nothing, grass for example, and weave it into beautiful baskets or attractive sandals. One boy turned a scrap of wood from a broken Army pallet into a pair of beautifully hand-carved high heels that Ruth wore off duty. But Ruth most admired the Filipino resilience she saw in their smiling faces. *They've suffered so much more than I ever have*, Ruth realized. *They are survivors.*

A few nights after the Nagasaki bombing, Ruth sat in a corner of the emergency room: a tent with a cement floor, where they triaged incoming casualties. She rested her head on her arms at an exam table, daydreaming.

It's too crazy, Ruth thought as she drifted into an imagined conversation with her sister Linda who laughed at the pretentiousness of the idea, *Ladies don't become doctors. No one will ever marry you if you do that. Who do you think you are, anyway?* The string of Linda's likely arguments echoed in her head.

She's probably right, she imagined Anna joining in. *A doctor is no job for a woman—everyone says so. And you were lousy in school, how could you manage medical school? Forget about it.*

Interrupting her thoughts, she heard a man yelling, "Lieutenant, we have an injured soldier. Can you look at him?" Ruth jerked up, looking into the face of a tall man, dirty from the jungle. Two men, one with sergeant stripes, followed behind him carrying an injured man on a stretcher.

"Put him on the table," she said, now fully awake. "What happened?" she asked as the medic joined them.

"He tried to disarm a booby trap. It seemed fine, but then the grenade went off as he walked away from it," the tall man explained. "Our medic cleaned him up and wrapped him, so we carried him here, since you have all the best doctors in this area."

"Did they give him morphine?" the tent's medic asked.

All three shrugged.

The medic turned to Ruth. "Lieutenant, I think we've gotta assume their medic gave him a shot. I know I always give it if I have it. Anyway, he's passed out, so I don't think you should give him any."

Ruth nodded in agreement as she cut away the wounded man's pants and unwrapped the bandages around his leg and foot to examine the wounds. Seeing the puffy red and darkening tissue, Ruth felt an urgency to get him to surgery.

The medic took his vitals. "He has a temperature, and his blood pressure is high," he said as he wrote down the numbers on a card. Ruth suspected shrapnel trapped under the skin. She added further notes to the patient card as the medic handed her a syringe of penicillin.

He'll be lucky to keep that leg, Ruth thought, but she said, "We'll get him over to prep for surgery, Captain," noticing the rank of the man who'd woken her up. He nodded. His angular face was frozen in a tight grimace.

The medic signaled to the Filipinos who carried the stretcher over to pre-op as the medic ran alongside them.

"Hey, what about our stretcher?" the sergeant yelled.

"Dave, that is the least of our problems. Procure another one," the Captain answered using the ambiguous word that meant anything from outright theft to ordering from the supply system. Ruth suppressed a laugh, thinking what the sergeant would do to get another stretcher.

"Don't forget to tell them we think he already had morphine," Ruth yelled after the medic, who waved his hand in acknowledgement.

"You think he'll be okay?" the Captain asked.

Ruth had seen casualties fade away when she thought they would recover. She had learned not to promise anything. "I hope so," she said. "The doctors will take good care of him."

SEPTEMBER 1945

At the beginning of September, Ruth saw a spike in the number of soldiers suffering from tropical diseases, like scrub typhus, a common disease in the jungle and as bad as malaria. She kept her battered green medical dictionary close at hand in her knapsack at the nursing station to study unfamiliar conditions. But she wondered what good all this knowledge of tropical diseases would do for her back in Michigan.

One night as Ruth flipped through her dictionary, she saw an officer in a pressed tan uniform, walking toward her.

"Hi, Lieutenant, remember me?"

She didn't. *What does he want?* she asked herself, suspicious. He outranked her, but she was too tired to play the Army game of standing up for a senior officer, and anyway, he did not belong in her ward.

"Listen, Captain," she said, "you can't just walk into a sick ward whenever you like. What do you want?"

"I guess you don't remember me. You treated one of my men a few weeks ago. I'm Captain Rich Navarro, and I just wanted to thank you. He's doing fine, by the way. He won't be back to our outfit, but he's on his way home. He lost part of his foot, but the doc says he should be able to adjust back home."

"Oh, I remember—the booby trap case. Glad he made it." Ruth felt embarrassed she had been so gruff, and remembered to add, "Captain."

"Rich. You can call me Rich. I know you medical types don't think much of our Army rules, do you? And now that the war is ending, let's drop the formalities." He smiled. "Your name is Ruth, right? I, I mean, my unit, would like to invite you and the others who helped care for our man to a dinner at our officers' mess. We have some terrific cooks. If you're game, we'll pick you up. Just tell me when and how many. I'll send someone over tomorrow to make the arrangements."

A few days later, Ruth, the medic from the emergency room, Alice, and Lieutenant Wilson, who felt she should monitor the event, jumped at the chance to eat in his officers' mess. Four in all. There would have been more, but Ruth thought bringing too many would look bad.

Soon they sat down to a steak and potatoes dinner that reminded Ruth of dinners back home before the war.

"How can you have steak?" Wilson asked Rich.

"We always have it. We need to keep the boys fed for the patrols into the jungle, plus we have a great supply, sergeant. Not like yours," Rich laughed.

"What do you mean?" Wilson asked, interested.

"Everyone knows he's black-marketing food, especially the nurses', trading it away for booze and delicacies for his buddies and buying favors. He didn't get that fat on regular chow. And I hear he fancies himself to be quite a ladies' man, too. Seems to think he has the looks to be a movie actor after the war. He ingratiates himself with all the USO entertainers. I'd say he puts on quite a performance, but I don't see him as a leading man. Playing the heavy, you know, the gangster type, that would be more suited to him," Rich laughed again, along with the others who overheard the story.

Ruth noticed Lieutenant Wilson pursed her mouth into a look of angry determination, before she said, "That's very interesting, Captain."

Ruth detested the loud, overbearing supply sergeant. "It doesn't surprise me," she told Wilson. "We starve while he grows his pot belly stealing food meant for us." But Wilson just nodded, distracted.

Within days, she heard the supply sergeant had been reassigned to a medical unit going to the Hiroshima area on a special assignment. Ruth marveled at Wilson's ingenuity. When a fresh, by-the-book supply sergeant relieved him, the quality and quantity of the nurses' food immediately improved, even though some, like Colonel Bateman, were unhappy the supply of good booze disappeared.

OCTOBER 1945
Ruth felt sweat dripping down her back. Her long pants and long sleeves protected her against the malaria-carrying mosquitoes, but she felt hot inside the hospital tent packed with casualties. She sat doodling on a piece of paper, making lists of things she and Rich could do before they shipped out, going their separate ways. Since September they spent every free moment together and she had loved his company as they rode around in his jeep, enjoying movies, dances, USO shows, dinners at the officers' mess, and ballgames—all designed to keep the troops occupied while they waited to go home.

She massaged her knee. The aching signaled a weather change. In the rainy season that meant more rain, more mud. The ward holding two long rows of patients against each side smelled of wet, moldy canvas after months in the tropics.

Ruth studied the Dutchman, now looking less skeletal than when he first arrived. Ruth recalled how he had reacted to the Japanese prisoner of war with sadness but no malice. Arrowgoto, as the hospital staff called him, seemed content to remain with their unit forever.

The Dutchman often slept during the day and remained alert through the night. Ruth saw him smile at her and wave from his cot. She waved back. Ruth wondered when he would be evacuated, but the Army seemed to have forgotten all about him.

I wonder what the Dutchman has to go back to wherever he comes from. Maybe the Philippines is his home, Ruth was thinking, when Colonel Bateman rushed in looking agitated.

"Nurse," he yelled disregarding the sleeping patients. "I need to get into the medicine cabinet. Do you have the key?"

Ruth studied him as he fidgeted, making odd jerking motions. Since August, he had complained repeatedly about losing his practice in Chicago if the Army did not release him immediately. Many made arguments of why they needed to get home, especially after the Emperor surrendered, but Army policy required soldiers who were last in would be last out, so their unit expected to remain through the end of 1945 into early the next year.

"What do you need, Colonel?" Ruth asked, suspicious he wanted morphine. "If you give me the 'script, I'll get what you need for your patient. Which ward are you in? I'll bring it to you. Or Lieutenant Wilson will bring it over when she makes her rounds, if it is not an emergency."

"Dammit. You smartass nurses. You think you can talk to me this way? Open the medicine cabinet *now*. That's an order." He shook a fist in her face. Ruth felt angry he would try to hit her. Instead he ripped open her khaki shirt, the buttons popping off onto the ground. "Where's the key? I know you bitches keep the key in here," he said fishing around in her bra. Not finding anything made him angrier.

Ruth tried to squirm out of his reach. "Medic..." she started to shout when Bateman's hands squeezed around her neck.

"You will give me the key. I don't care if I have to kill you. You will give me the key."

Ruth gasped for breath. She felt dizzy and helpless. She tried to grab a pair of scissors on top of the table, but she could not reach them and she felt herself fading. *He is killing me*, she thought, as she slumped to the ground. Then she felt his grasp suddenly release and saw him fly up into the air before landing hard on the table, smashing its legs. *How did he manage to do that?* Ruth wondered.

The next day, Ruth felt a mix of pity and satisfaction at seeing Colonel Bateman strapped tight into a straitjacket then tied to the top of a canvas covered Army truck frame so people could not see the colonel as he thrashed helplessly and screamed over and over, "My practice, my practice, I'll kill you!"

Ruth overheard the guards laughing as they talked to the driver, waiting for the medic who would ride in the back of the truck to make sure the colonel did not hurt himself before they loaded him onto the evacuation aircraft. "That crazy colonel can scream as much as he likes, as long as I get a free ride to Honolulu," one soldier said. Ruth did not envy the Army Air Force flight nurse on that trip.

"If that Dutchman hadn't intervened, I don't know what would have happened to you," Ruth heard Wilson saying to her as the truck drove away. "I knew Bateman drank a lot, but how did he get addicted to morphine? It's a wonder he functioned in the operating room," she remarked, not expecting an answer. "I'm glad you stood your ground, Ruth, but he's twice your size. He could have killed you."

"Good riddance to him," Ruth said vaguely, still feeling the angry shock of the attack, her body aching. "Maybe he'll recover his senses in the psych ward. I imagine he'll end up in a padded cell." She spoke with indifference. "Are you sure it was the Dutchman?"

"No one is talking. When they tried to interview the soldiers last night half of them claimed they personally attacked the colonel. Even the guy in traction said he did it. One guy claimed he saw the soldier in a coma get up and fly across the tent to knock the colonel down. The other half claim they didn't see or hear a thing because they were sleeping so soundly, which I don't believe for a minute. We all heard the racket."

Ruth started laughing. "Oh, you think it's funny," Wilson said, laughing along with her. "Anyway, we all decided to drop the whole thing. Too much paperwork to sort it out and it would make the unit look bad. We gave the colonel a line of duty letter for his injuries. He'll probably get a Purple Heart and never remember why. We thought it best to send him on his way."

"What will happen to the Dutchman?" Ruth asked, hoping he would not be arrested.

"Nothing. No one wants to tackle this mess. How would we write it up? He shouldn't still be here. They're talking about moving him over to the Red Cross hospital before we leave."

"I hope they find a good place for him. I hate to leave him with his situation unresolved when we ship out," Ruth said.

Wilson was quick to respond. "He's lucky he didn't kill the colonel. They would have arrested him for sure, maybe even executed him the way things are going. Some of the guys say he knew exactly what he was doing when he broke the colonel's hold around your neck and threw him onto the table. Some think he's had commando training, but everyone's calling him a hero, so we're letting it drop."

NOVEMBER 1945

A large spider crawled across the desk where Ruth wrote her charts on each patient. She deftly knocked it off onto the ground, remembering how she'd screamed the first time she saw one back in June. Like her fellow nurses, Ruth now casually brushed aside or bashed spiders and snakes with whatever was at hand as efficiently as she cared for her patients. Even the rats running over the frame of her mosquito net at night or darting along the ground no longer bothered her.

"The rats have become part of the furniture," Lieutenant Wilson liked to say. "As long as they don't eat the patients, I have no quarrel with them anymore."

"Ruth, when do you think they'll let us leave here?" Alice asked, knowing it would be sometime after New Year's.

"Why? Are you in a hurry to get out of here? You might be able to go out in a straitjacket," Ruth teased.

"Very funny. I just want to go somewhere else—anywhere," Alice answered, sounding depressed.

"What happened to that engineer you were dating? I thought you intended to marry him," Ruth asked.

"I did, but someone already beat me to it. He has a family back in the States. Jerk. He lied to me. I had to find out from one of his buddies. At least Rich is straight with you that he's married," Alice said, making Ruth blush that she was going out with a married man. "Is he going to divorce her?"

"That's what he says," Ruth said feeling uneasy. "Sometimes I wish I never got involved with him."

"He's handsome and charming. Who can blame you?" Alice observed. "If he had paid attention to me like he does to you, I might have fallen for him. Enjoy it. Even if it doesn't come to anything, you're having fun now, aren't you?"

"Yes." Ruth lit up, smiling. "He makes me feel special. He's always been a gentleman."

"A gentleman, huh? Be careful that isn't a ploy to get you into bed then dump you. He might like the chase," Alice said.

Ruth wanted to say she'd be careful, but she wondered if she could.

DECEMBER 1945

After the news finished on the radio, Ruth heard the angry grumbles of soldiers complaining about the slow pace of ships returning to the States. No one wanted to admit that the volume of returning solders stretched the logistics system and that some soldiers caused delays. Ruth found it hard to understand how an Army that defeated the Axis Powers in Europe and the Pacific could unravel with some soldiers disobeying orders, even abandoning their vehicles at port, causing delays in loading the ships to take people home. The erosion of military discipline created a vicious cycle of bottlenecks that added more time and fueled more frustration. *We're lucky the Japanese prisoners haven't taken advantage of this mess*, Ruth thought.

With Bing Crosby's voice crooning "White Christmas," Ruth thought, *This is just what we need*, as she fought to control a wave of depression. She saw the song affecting the men. Some turned their heads away from her while she made her rounds, not wanting her to see them cry, or swearing to cover up their emotions.

"Nurse! Lieutenant? Ma'am? Do you have a weapon to kill that fucking radio!" a soldier yelled from the back corner of the ward.

"Hey, watch your language, soldier," a medic yelled before Ruth could say anything. "You're still in the Army and talking to an officer! You'd better learn how to talk like a civilized human being again before you go home. Your women won't appreciate your soldier talk."

Ruth said nothing but walked over to the radio and abruptly turned it off.

"Thank you, ma'am!" a soldier yelled as a chorus of clapping arose throughout the ward.

Back home Ruth had loved that old song, but in the tropical rain and mud of the Philippines in December it pierced with longing and sadness. It made Ruth ache for the white snows back home.

Ruth had no memory of Norman Rockwell family scenes around Christmas dinner. Of necessity, Christmas celebrations were lean affairs. Consequently, Ruth's yearning for Christmas had less to do with nostalgia for something lost, and more to do with wanting to feel cool. She also dreamed of a future creating her own family dinners with a good husband and children. Ruth decided having a large family like her mother had meant poverty and denied opportunities. It also created endless, backbreaking housework. The only clear image Ruth had of her mother, who died in her early forties, was seeing her working like a charwoman and turning her meager pantry into enough to feed her hungry family.

I don't want that, Ruth thought. Instead, she dreamed of having two boys and two girls, closely spaced so they would all enjoy their childhood together. *That way,* Ruth reasoned, *each will have a good friend.*

Mid-daydream, Ruth was startled to see First Lieutenant Wilson rush into the tent. In the eight months that had passed since they boarded the *Lurline,* they had become close friends and used first names. Esther looked tired and drained.

Esther has aged, Ruth thought, wondering how much she had as well. Then she worried Esther might be coming down with TB or a tropical disease. She had been spending a lot of time in the infectious wards.

"Will I see you at the baseball games over New Year's?" Wilson asked.

Ruth hesitated, knowing Esther would not like her plans. "I have a pass. Rich and I plan to stay at the officers' club in Manila."

Esther looked shocked, her eyebrows rising. "You're going to spend the night with that captain? You know, he's no good. He's one of those married playboys. You deserve better," she bluntly told Ruth.

Ruth felt angry. Whether it was at herself or Esther she was not sure, but she shot back, "It's none of your business who I go around with. I think I love him. And he says he loves me."

"Oh, Ruth," Esther said, shaking her head.

CHAPTER 7

LIKE NOTHING HAPPENED

(JANUARY – JUNE 1946)

JANUARY 1946

With the rush to send soldiers home before Christmas, those who remained, like Ruth, felt a need to celebrate Christmas and New Year's with special food and music. The supply sergeant turned the Christmas dinner into a feast of extra turkeys, dressing, cranberries, red and green Jell-O salads, potatoes, canned vegetables, and local fruit for the hospital team, including Filipino nurses and staff. They also arranged a party for the children of the area, many of whom had become orphans during liberation. Everyone ate well and insisted the Filipino men and women take the bulk of the food back to their families and communities. Ruth felt it a nice way to end their tour in the Philippines. Although she understood one meal was not enough, it helped make Christmas 1945 special for the Filipinos.

After Ruth finished eating, she watched Alice dancing toward her wearing a floppy grass hat, swaying to a live band of Filipinos playing American swing music. "Isn't this great? They sound just like Duke Ellington's band, but they can do anything—Benny Goodman, Count Basie, you name it. I don't know how but they sound just like them. It's amazing."

"They are great. I love live music. I miss going to clubs in Detroit. We had a lot of fun dancing," Ruth said.

"Where's your captain? Why didn't he come to our party?" Alice asked.

"I'm meeting him in Manila on Saturday to watch the start of the baseball series and I'll stay with him over New Year's," Ruth said.

"So, this is it. You're getting serious. I heard Rich volunteered to stay on longer if they let him. What will you do?" Alice said.

"He thinks he'll be back in Hawaii next spring. He wants me to join him there."

"What about his wife and children?" Alice asked.

"He says he'll divorce her and then we can get married. He says his marriage was over a long time ago," Ruth said.

Alice said nothing but looked puzzled. Ruth did not really care what Alice thought, though she could not help asking her, "What are you thinking?"

"Oh, just that that's what they all say, and then there is the fact that he's Catholic, Ruth. Did you know that? He can't get a divorce. Maybe he can get an annulment, but that would make his children illegitimate. Are you sure about this?"

With no hesitation Ruth said, "Yes." Even so, she felt doubts crowding her thoughts. She did know he was Catholic and he couldn't divorce, but she had pushed that out of her mind when Rich said he would divorce his wife, so she believed it would work out.

Mother would be so disappointed with me if she had lived, Ruth thought. She felt confused and sad, but remembered Anna had become Catholic for Frank. *Times are changing. Why should religion keep people who love each other apart?* she reasoned to herself.

The rest of the week went by in a blur as Ruth found herself daydreaming arguments with her sisters. She knew she could not change her religion. She wondered if Rich would change his. And what about children? If he did not convert, would he insist their children be raised Catholic?

By the time she met Rich in Manila just before the competition started, Ruth had worked herself into a state of doubt. Maybe Esther and Alice were right, but when she saw Rich smiling and looking charming in his dress uniform, she tried to suppress her negative thoughts.

As they walked over to the baseball field, Rich ran ahead to look for a good spot in the officers' bleachers. Ruth lagged behind, thinking of the first time she saw the city. Wreckage remained, but she felt Manila coming back to life.

Maybe they can recover and become the Pearl of the Orient again, she hoped.

Ruth heard someone yell her name. As she studied the crowd of military streaming toward the field, Ruth thought she saw Joe Walker approaching her. She hadn't seen him since they were kids and thought it must be someone who just looked like him. The man walking toward her swaggered like a soldier. He looked muscular and confident in his khaki uniform, with his golden-brown face framed in short black hair. His garrison cap stuck out of his pants pocket, as if daring someone to tell him to put his hat on. Competent, but rebellious. That had to be Joe.

They rushed up to each other but did not touch. Ruth felt self-conscious. Joe looked uncertain, then held out his hand and they shook, not speaking for a while.

"It sure is good to see you, Ruth. You look great," Joe said, staring at her.

"Eddie told me you were out this way, but I never thought I would see you. I had no idea you were in Manila," Ruth responded, fidgeting with her purse that hung over her left shoulder.

"I figured you were here when I got a letter from Eddie and he said you were heading this way back in April. I knew they were building up hospital units and thought you might be part of that. I always hoped I would run into you. Where have you been?"

"I was here for about a month after we arrived in May, then we moved down to Batangas. I still can't believe I ran into you," Ruth exclaimed.

"All the units that are left seem to be here for the baseball series and New Year's, so maybe it's not so crazy. It sure is great to see someone from home," Joe said smiling, which reminded Ruth that he loved to play baseball.

"Where have you been?" Ruth asked.

"It feels like everywhere. I landed on Leyte before MacArthur. Then Lingayen Gulf. No resistance. We were so lucky. We kept thinking the Japanese would attack, but they didn't. They made up for it in Manila, though. That was tough. My unit followed them up into the hills to ferret them out one hole at a time. They are some tough fighters. They fight to the death like warriors."

Ruth nodded. By now she had pieced together what had happened and how ugly the fighting became when the Japanese realized they could not win. Many kept on until they were killed or committed suicide. Ruth admired their tenacity too, but the atrocities they committed disturbed her.

"Were you injured?" Ruth asked.

"Not a scratch." He pulled out his hat and showed Ruth an eagle feather. "See this? I was smart for a change. I got it blessed by an elder before I left the U.P. It saved me more times than I can count."

Rich emerged through the growing crowd and pressed close to Ruth's side, grabbing her right arm possessively.

Joe shot a look at the arm, ignoring Rich until he said, "How are you, Sergeant? Do you know the Lieutenant?"

Ruth and Joe mirrored their astonishment, realizing each other's rank. Then, Joe spoke. "Yes, sir. We grew up together back in northern Michigan."

"Really? She's told me about the north. It sounds primitive," Rich scoffed. "Ruth, they're holding seats for us on the officers' side."

Ruth saw the anger building in Joe, just like when he was a boy facing down a bully. She hoped he would not do anything and resisted Rich's tug, wanting to talk a bit longer.

"When are you leaving?" Ruth asked, disengaging her arm from Rich.

"My outfit ships out in a couple of days. I am heading back to Bay Mills as soon as I can get there. I can't wait to walk through the woods and sit along the lake. I may walk all the way over to see Eddie and Mary." He smiled, seeming to think about how he would do that and how long it would take on foot.

"I'm heading home in a couple of weeks," Ruth said, as if she'd just made up her mind. She noticed Rich stiffen next to her. "If you see them before I do, please tell them I'm fine."

"Will do," Joe affirmed, still smiling.

"Maybe I'll see you in the U.P.," Ruth suggested, regretting she was with Rich and regretting she was an officer, wishing she and Joe could take a walk and talk about the war and all the death and damage they'd seen and what it meant until it didn't hurt so much anymore.

"Have a safe journey home. The ship will be much faster now that they don't need to avoid subs." Joe smiled again, waving to them as he turned around and headed for the enlisted bleachers to watch the game.

"Disrespectful jerk," Rich muttered, "I should have him brought up on charges."

"For what?" Ruth asked, almost laughing.

"He wasn't wearing his hat, he didn't salute, and he was too chummy with you," Rich said, his face darkening.

When Ruth was seated next to Rich, he spitted out, "How do you know that Indian, anyway?"

"We went to school together as kids in Big Bay, and later in Marquette for a while."

"Come on. Don't they ship the Indians away to schools where they can learn how to be civilized and speak English?"

Ruth felt her anger rising. "He did get shipped to a school for a while and he worked in a CCC camp. He had a rough life. Lost his father, then they took him away from his mother."

"Sounds like a sad case," Rich said indifferently. "I heard from a buddy that some of those people earned their keep over here talking their Indian mumbo jumbo." He looked over to where Joe found a seat. "You see that guy with him? The one he's talking to. I'll bet he was assigned to kill him if the enemy got too close. You know, better a dead Indian." Rich laughed.

Ruth had no idea what he was talking about, but she felt malice as Rich's mask fell revealing his real face—mean, arrogant, and selfish. Later, as they watched the game, he pressed her to meet him in Hawaii so they could be together while he worked on his wife for a divorce. But she knew he was a liar. As she excused herself to use the latrine, she felt free of him and kept walking until she found a ride back to Batangas.

The next day Ruth decided to forget her pass and go back to work in the ward. It was better than sitting around in her tent.

When she entered the tent ward, a medic yelled, "Lieutenant Amundsen! I thought we wouldn't see you for a few more days. Something is wrong with the Dutchman. He's supposed to go with the Red Cross representatives here," he pointed to a couple of people standing looking at their watches, "but he refuses to budge. I've never had this problem with him before. He may not talk, but he's always been cooperative. We could try to carry him, but he's pretty big. I don't want to call the MPs. What should I do?"

"Let me try," Ruth said walking over to the Dutchman's cot, where he sat with his back turned toward the medic. As she stood next to him, she smiled, realizing they appeared to be the same height. He noticed her and smiled too, seeming to relax, so she sat next to him. Ruth felt he had been waiting for her, and she was glad she came back early.

Ruth always talked to him like nothing was wrong, believing acting normal would help him somehow. She said, "You know, I never thanked you properly for saving my life. Bateman would have killed me if you hadn't helped me. Thank you."

At his silence, she continued talking. "It's time for you to go now. You can't stay here. We're leaving soon and who knows what will happen to you, so you should go with the Red Cross. They might be able to help you find your people, and you still need some medical care that they can provide. Understand?"

The Dutchman nodded, seeming to understand what she said. Then he spoke in accented but clear English, "Thank you, Lieutenant Amundsen. It has been a pleasure. I wish you nothing but the best." He stood up, bending down to shake her hand, as she sat there too stunned to answer. He walked over to the Red Cross personnel. As they left together, the Dutchman turned and smiled at Ruth and gave her a little wave.

A couple weeks later, Alice, Esther, and Ruth sat in their cabin on a ship heading back to San Francisco, crowded together playing hearts and drinking shapely bottles of Coca-Cola.

"Tell me again, Ruth. You mean that sneaky bastard could speak all along and in English no less? He sure played us for fools," Alice said.

"We protected him," Esther sighed. "Maybe he was a communist after all."

Ruth said, "I'd like to think he just recovered from shock under our care. Who knows? Maybe the incident with Bateman woke him up, but he waited until he left to speak, out of courtesy."

"Courtesy?" Alice laughed. "You always thought him a gentleman. Maybe he's a gentleman communist. But what does talking have to do with manners?"

"He didn't want to upset us," Ruth said.

"Maybe he just didn't want to leave. He had a sweet deal with us," Alice said. "Well, I guess we'll never know his story, but I think we should toast him." She stood, raising a bottle. "To the Dutchman."

Ruth and Esther stood as they chorused, "To the Dutchman."

JUNE 1946

Ruth's wool uniform felt hot and sticky in the warming weather as she waited on the sunny platform for the train from Detroit to Marquette. She promised Eddie and Mary she would wear it, but she felt funny in it now, even though discharged men still wore their uniforms. She looked forward to the solitude of the private coach she'd splurged on to think about the future.

"Hey, toots," a man whistled. "Are you a ticket taker?" He was laughing and swaying from too much alcohol as he leered at her sitting on a bench on the platform, looking her up and down like an item for purchase.

"No," Ruth said, controlling her anger at his reference to her Army nurse uniform. She wanted to say more but cautioned herself. *Ignore him. Too many bastards these days.* She thought of how the end of the war had unleashed something cruel in people as peace cast aside common effort. She pegged him for a veteran. *Enlisted,* Ruth thought, studying his shoes. *Probably in trouble most of the time.*

Almost five months since she'd left the Philippines and the Army, Ruth felt disconnected from civilian life in postwar America. *How can I feel so different after only a year in uniform?* Ruth wondered. During the war, Ruth felt respect and appreciation. Back home now, these thoughts seemed delusional as she felt people saw her as just another dame. The layer of protection she felt as an officer now stripped away in the rush to get back to what everyone told her was "normal."

Ruth saw a tall woman, *a former WAC*, Ruth judged from her bearing, watching the conversation. After the drunk left, she approached Ruth. She looked uncomfortable in a prim dress with matching heels, her purse stuck at an odd angle under her arm. She told Ruth, "You're asking for trouble in your uniform, Lieutenant. Be careful. Some men around here think it means you're available."

Her warning upset Ruth because of its truth. With the war over, Ruth found women's accomplishments in uniform undervalued—even erased. Many seemed to want to forget the war. Civilian women could be particularly vicious too, looking down on women veterans with a mixture of envy and suspicion. The men who did not go overseas during the war were worse. It seemed the women who served overseas made them feel less a man, and they resented it.

Ruth moved over to the train. She smiled at the porter, a Black man, feeling relieved to see a kind face as he offered his hand to help Ruth step up into the train. Studying her Second Lieutenant rank, nursing insignia, and ribbons, he smiled and said, "Welcome aboard, Lieutenant."

After Ruth settled into her cabin and the train moved away from the station the porter stood outside her open door to check her ticket. "Where did you serve, ma'am?" he asked.

Not accustomed to being asked anything about her service, Ruth hesitated. "I was in a general hospital unit in the Philippines—Manila and Batangas. Did you serve?"

"Yes. I was in Italy. A few of the other guys on board served in the Pacific. I think our Army guy was in the China-Burma-India theater. The Marine guy was at Iwo Jima. He was supposed to help offload the ship, but things got too hot too fast and he had to fight for his life alongside the regular troops. Bad luck, I guess, but he made it out." He laughed. Then becoming serious, he said, "You know, we all appreciated what the nurses did for us. We didn't always have Black nurses around, and you cared for us just the same. We appreciated that."

"Boy! Are you bothering this lady?" a heavy-set, red-faced train conductor yelled at the porter.

Ruth saw anger flash quickly over the porter's face, then vanish into a perfunctory smile. "No, sir. The Lieutenant here served in the Pacific."

The white man crowded into the compartment, pressing into the gap between Ruth and the porter. "Is he bothering you, ma'am?"

"Oh, no," Ruth replied. She smelled onions on his breath. "We were just talking about the war. Where did you serve?" Ruth asked, betting he hadn't left this train during the war.

"Ah, I was mission essential, you know," he said. "George! You'd better get along and finish taking tickets."

After they left, Ruth closed the door tight, studying how the door locked. She did not like the look or smell of the conductor.

As Ruth settled back into her seat, she felt old. Weary. She would turn twenty-six in October. The faces of the soldiers she had cared for weighed on her. Worse, her memories of the women and children haunted her. Their smiling faces appeared in her dreams, small hands reaching out to beg for food or hustle a trinket. She smiled, remembering the first time they held out luscious mangoes they collected from the ground. *I doubt I will find any mangoes here.* Ruth sighed. *What did it all mean for me? And what good is my wartime experience now?*

Ruth sighed again, realizing she would never be able to explain how she felt to people who hadn't been there. She understood what the boys went through in their brutal jungle warfare across the Pacific. But civilians, she was learning, held distorted ideas of the war and the victory. Ruth felt a growing chasm between herself and them, and with the girl she had been before the war. She found it difficult to talk about it with anyone.

Anyway, the civilians act uninterested, she thought. Even her sister, Anna, whom Ruth visited in February following her discharge at Fort Sam Houston, found nothing to say. Anna asked a few questions, then changed the subject before Ruth answered, preferring to talk about a new recipe or dress style.

Ruthie, you need to get some new clothes while you're here. My treat, Anna had offered, perhaps feeling a little guilty that she did not want to know what Ruth did or saw in the Philippines.

Back when the war ended in August, soldiers began to talk about what they could tell their families. Some thought World War I veterans and those that had served in Europe would understand, but talking to civilians would be impossible. Worse, those who served in the military safe inside the States seemed to carry a chip on their shoulders trying to rationalize why they never went overseas.

Ruth remembered a sad burn case: a sergeant she'd cared for before she left Batangas. As she changed his dressings, he asked her, *Nurse, what am I going to tell my wife and children about how I got burned?*

After coming through multiple engagements with the enemy without a scratch, the sergeant had been burned in a fight with his Filipina mistress when he told her he was shipping out and could not take her back to the States. The fight escalated until the desperate woman threw gasoline on him and set him on fire. His buddies saved him, but he became depressed.

I don't know, Ruth had replied, shaking her head, feeling a mix of pity and sadness for his wife and family. When he died two days later, Ruth was convinced he gave up on life rather than face his shame.

As she watched the scenery go by, Ruth felt absence. She missed Alice, who went back to California, and Esther, who remained in the service. As they scattered, they promised to keep in touch, but Ruth knew that would be hard. Margaret also remained on active duty working in the Army's "Operation War Bride," ferrying wives and children of servicemen from Europe across the Atlantic.

The week before Ruth left the Philippines, she'd received a letter from Margaret, which she pulled out now and re-read as she settled into the rhythm of the train. Margaret wrote how she felt like a glorified babysitter, changing diapers and babysitting, as shipload after shipload of women and children crossed the Atlantic. After serving as a flight nurse evacuating wounded and shell shock cases from England to Walter Reed Hospital in Washington, D.C., Margaret wrote she felt her nursing skills were being misused, but she also felt grateful to remain on active duty.

Unlike most Army nurses, including Ruth who had been pushed out in the rapid demobilization, Margaret stayed. *How did she and Esther manage to stay in?* Ruth thought with envy. Margaret even had a plan; she said she would play along with the babysitting mission and transfer to the War Bride operation in the Pacific. From there she hoped to go to Japan for the duration of the occupation. She had no plans to marry. *I like the Army life*, Margaret said. *It suits me and drives my parents crazy.*

Ruth imagined Margaret laughing as she concluded her letter with, "After caring for all these babies and children, I have no interest in having my own." Then she added, "There are so many orphans, maybe I can find a way to help them."

The train circled around the western side of Lake Michigan, passing through Chicago and Milwaukee. Ruth felt a lightness when they left the cities behind. As she watched the trees replace buildings, Ruth looked forward to spending time with her cousin Eddie and his wife Mary, who had invited her to visit. Eddie wanted to show her off in her uniform so he could properly welcome her home as a returning war hero at the station. Did he know he would be the only one to do that for Ruth?

Some men who still wore their uniforms lacked civilian clothes or the money to buy them. But many felt reluctant to strip off their identities as victors, enjoying their honored guest treatment wherever they went in the heady months after V-E and V-J days. Strangers patted them on the back and gave boisterous "thank yous." They provided free drinks and meals and encouraged the men to tell stories of their adventures in the war. Before the Black train porter, no one had yet thanked Ruth or asked her what she did.

After she left the Philippines, the only time Ruth felt appreciated was on the troop train from San Francisco to Texas, when soldiers boisterously thanked the nurses even while they eyed them up as potential brides. "Sure, the doc stitched me up, but I never would have made it," many said, "without the care of a nurse."

Ruth knew women were not the only veterans in uniform who did not get respect as the unity of the country evaporated and old ideas about everyone's place reemerged. Among the worst, Ruth had heard back in February while she out-processed at Fort Sam Houston, that a Black Army veteran in uniform, Sergeant Isaac Woodard, had been beaten blind by the North Carolina police while he rode a bus home. The incident created a national outrage and President Truman ordered a federal investigation, but everyone knew Woodard would get no justice. He certainly would never see again. Ruth saw the incident as a warning to anyone who might try to step out of line—a fact emphasized in the way the conductor treated the porter.

In the months after the war ended while still in the Philippines, many nurses rushed to make up time by marrying doctors and other servicemen. Before the war, Ruth would have been shocked that people would marry so quickly, but now she thought it made sense. Why wait? With so many men gone forever, killed in the war, many felt a sense of imbalance and urgency to settle down quickly with the eligible men that remained. Ruth thought marrying a fellow serviceman offered some shared understanding and experiences that she thought she could never find with a civilian.

After Ruth broke it off with Rich and returned to the States, however, she'd wanted some time to herself. She got her job back at the Henry Ford Hospital in Detroit after visiting Anna, who wanted Ruth to stay with her. But Ruth did not feel at home in Oklahoma. Ruth felt restless. She knew more than anything she wanted to keep working, but she felt adrift without her war friends. She especially missed the pace and challenge of the work. *What am I going to do now?* Ruth asked herself.

Margaret's letter about going to Japan made Ruth wonder if she could re-enter the Army Nurse Corps. At Fort Sam

Houston they said to check back in a few years and maybe something would open up, but Ruth wanted to act now. She felt adrift in peacetime America. After rationing ended and the feared Depression had not re-emerged, people seemed crazy to buy anything. Manufacturing shifted from guns and ammunition to washing machines, refrigerators, and other products. Ruth found this unsettling, especially knowing that people in the Philippines had so little.

The greeting Ruth received at the Marquette station made her feel special. Eddie and Mary stood front and center with flowers and a bottle of champagne. Eddie was waving his arms wildly. "There she is! There's our hero!"

Eddie took Ruth's bag to their car, talking quickly. "Joe said you looked grand in your uniform and he sure was right."

"Did he really walk all the way here from Bay Mills?" Ruth asked.

"He did. He said he had a great time. He's talking about going back to school or going up to Alaska," Mary said.

"What's up in Alaska?" Ruth asked.

"Wilderness. More trees and wild animals, like grizzlies," Mary laughed.

As they drove up the road from Marquette to Big Bay, Eddie's car skidded at times on the gravel curves. Ruth said, "Man, I missed this place."

"Why don't you come back up here, then? Why stay in Detroit?" Eddie asked.

"I like working in Detroit. It is exciting and the cases that come into the hospital are more like what I saw in the Philippines. I feel like I'm doing something of value. Saving lives. But I do worry about marriage and children. I'm almost twenty-six and my youth is slipping away, you know."

"Oh, that's people talking, Ruthie, not you. You have plenty of time if that is what you want. Don't let them push you," Mary said.

Once in the cabin guest room, Ruth changed out of her uniform, carefully packing it into her suitcase to minimize wrinkling. She put on a worn flannel shirt, pants, and walking shoes.

"I need to see the lake," Ruth announced to Mary and Eddie as she walked into the kitchen.

Eddie said, "I thought you might want to get that jungle and city air out of your system. Let's take the old trail through the white pine grove. Are you ready, Mary?" Eddie looked at his wife then to Ruth, adding, "She's made some sandwiches for us to take on our walk. We thought we'd sit on one of those big rocks on the shoreline where there's a breeze to blow away the bugs."

"That sounds great," Ruth answered. They walked out of the cabin, Eddie carrying a woven wood picnic basket with a red and white checkered linen tablecloth covering the open top.

The three of them walked through the trail, winding through the old growth of white pine, each tree towering above them like a cathedral.

"Just imagine what it must have been like when these trees covered the whole area," Ruth said in wonder.

"It would have been hard to develop a country if we left it covered in these grand trees, though, don't you think," said Mary.

"At least we have a sanctuary for them here," added Eddie.

Ruth almost fell over bending backward to look up to see the tops of the white pine as they walked through the grove to Lake Superior.

"How tall are these trees?" Ruth asked.

"Over a hundred feet, but the old growth can go up to two hundred feet," Eddie said.

"That's unbelievable," Ruth said with awe.

"Just think how large those giant sequoias can get in California. Imagine. They can reach more than three hundred feet. I would sure like to get out there to see them sometime," Mary added. Like Eddie, she was an avid outdoorsperson with practical knowledge of flora, especially trees.

"Will Rogers said he never met a man he didn't like, but I say that about trees, especially these beauties. Just think about the times they've lived through," Eddie mused. As they reached the shoreline, they stopped to look out across Lake Superior. "And then there's this view. Pretty special, eh, Ruth?"

Ruth stared north toward Canada; a lake freighter passed in the distance, heading west toward Duluth. "It is special."

Later, as they walked back to the cabin, Eddie asked, "What did you think of that book, *The Razor's Edge*?"

"I think I understand him and why, after being rich and throwing that lifestyle away, he decided to spend his life as a cab driver helping people to get around."

"It gave him time to keep learning, too. Not a bad way to spend your life," said Eddie.

"Oh, you two philosophers," Mary teased them. Then turning to Eddie, she asked, "So where's your inheritance from your rich uncle?" Ruth and Mary laughed.

"Very funny. No, I mean his search to understand why we are here."

"A fool's errand, if you ask me," Mary said.

"Mm. All I know is when I am in a place like here in the woods or on Lake Superior," Ruth declared, "I feel like I have all the answers I need."

"You should be a naturalist roaming the woods, Ruthie. What more could anyone want?" Eddie asked, waving his hands around him at the forest.

Ruth shook her head, laughing, "I think our saloon keeper grandfather would be surprised to know that two of his grandchildren became such dreamers."

CHAPTER 8

THE CALL NORTH

(AUGUST – NOVEMBER 1946)

AUGUST 1946

Margaret surprised Ruth with a visit while home on leave to see her family near Detroit. Ruth had not seen her since they parted during training in early 1945. Fortunately, Ruth's day off fell in the middle of the week, so she had time to meet Margaret at Crowley's Department Store. They met for a late lunch when they thought it would be quiet for a long talk. The working lunch crowd had finished, but some tables of ladies drinking tea remained. They gave Ruth and Margaret hostile stares when they entered the restaurant.

"What's up with them?" Ruth said as she sat down.

"They probably think my pants are unladylike. Careful, they may be pegging us for deviants," Margaret laughed. "I'm surprised no one threw me out. I've been getting a lot of stares and head shaking. There seems to be an anti-pants campaign, didn't you know, to support the idea that women should be in the kitchen."

A waitress offered them a menu and returned to take their orders for club sandwiches, after serving them coffee.

"People can be so tiresome," Ruth said. "Sometimes I think it is not worth fighting them."

"Ruth, we must always fight them. That's one thing I learned from the war. If you give in or avoid confrontation, these people grow bolder and more powerful and the next thing you know, Hitler appears and you're left wondering where this monster came from and why we are fighting another war," Margaret said, waving her hands, which caught the eye of the tea drinkers, who, Ruth noticed, whispered and laughed at them.

Changing the subject, Ruth said, "Tell me about your work. What did you think of the Pacific? Did you make it to Manila?" Ruth leaned in, eager to hear Margaret's news.

"It is grand, as you know. After crossing the Atlantic umpteen times, the Pacific feels so much bigger! Water as far as you can see for days at a time. And the stars at night: I remember you writing me about them, but I had no idea how wonderful they are," Margaret said. "You know what I mean. You were there."

"I loved the salt air, too," Ruth said, thinking about her month-long crossing to Manila in 1945 and her much faster return in January.

"The work, as I wrote you, did not amount to much except changing diapers, babysitting, and an occasional illness or scrape. Although some of the women did need some extra care if you know what I mean."

"Malnutrition or something else?" Ruth asked, remembering the women who hustled GIs for money and food to live on.

"Malnutrition, yes, and some cases of tropical disease, and, you know, a few who needed VD treatment. Not many, but I felt sorry for them because people have so little and prostitution was a way to feed their family. Many were outcasts. I don't envy the road ahead for any of them in America, and the children will have a hard time, I think," Margaret added. "I did get to Manila. It was abuzz with construction and clean up. I did some sightseeing, but it is hard to imagine what it looked like before the war."

"What about Japan? Will you be able to go there?"

"Yes. I am taking a couple weeks off, then I'm getting some additional training in how to treat radiation burns. We know so little about the effects of the bombs, but it looks like the aftereffects could last for a long time. I also hope to work with some of the orphanages to treat those kids."

"It sounds exciting," Ruth said, a sense of longing entering her voice.

"Why don't you volunteer? They might even give you a higher rank. I think it is a great life, if you know how to make it work for you," Margaret said.

"You know I tried to stay in, but the Army didn't want me, and I don't see how that's any different after a few months. My sister, Anna, you know the one that moved to Tulsa during the war, wants me to come out there to work. My other sister, Linda, is begging me to help her. She has a small child and needs help until her husband comes back from the Pacific, which may be some time yet. How can I leave the country again?"

"You mean the sister up in the U.P.?" Margaret asked, incredulous.

"Yes, She's in Sault Ste. Marie. Her husband mobilized from the Coast Guard base there, so she stayed behind in town. She's had a rough time alone. She's hoping he will be reassigned back there soon."

"Really?" Margaret sounded skeptical. "That does not seem likely, does it? Why doesn't she move out to the West Coast to wherever his home port is? That would be better, wouldn't it? Anyway, what on earth are you going to do there? Do they even have a decent hospital up there? Lord, with your skills, you could work anywhere. Anyway, I thought you wanted to continue your education with the GI Bill and add a year to your studies, so you would have a four-year nursing degree. Maybe you could study anesthesiology. Or you even go to medical school like you wrote me. Why limit yourself after all you've seen and done?"

"Oh, Margaret, you make it sound so simple. You know things are not that easy for me. The town has a good hospital. Anyway, I want to have a family and I miss the U.P."

"Well, kid, you know I support you, but you and your damn U.P.! All they have up there are mosquitoes, huge flies, bears, replanted trees, and bars. That's no place for you. Not anymore. You can't be thinking of going back up north," Margaret said, throwing her hands up in frustration.

"It's home to me, Margaret."

The waitress arrived with their sandwiches, as the tea ladies haughtily got up, throwing nasty looks to Margaret on their way out. The waitress refreshed their coffee without asking and whisked away without a word.

Margaret studied Ruth's face, but said nothing. Ruth realized Margaret was assessing whether Ruth had already made up her mind. Seemingly wanting to change the subject, Margaret asked about work.

"How do you like working at Ford?"

"It's not the same as when we worked there before we joined the Army, but I see a lot of different cases. The doctors tend to ask for those of us who served overseas when they get tough ones. I guess they figure we can take it and keep our heads. One of my patients is a very young girl who looks underage, but already has several kids. She keeps coming back again and again for syphilis treatment. Poor thing, she can't understand how she gets it, since she only has relations with her husband. They came up here for war work. I don't think they have much education."

"Kissing cousins maybe," Margaret scoffed.

"The doctor tried to talk to the husband, but he threatened to beat the doctor and told him to mind his own business. He says he wants his wife fixed up once and for all since she's wasting so much of his money. I'm afraid he'll quit bringing her in, and she'll get sicker. Sad. I think the doctor will put social services on them, but I doubt it will help. Must be rough for those kids, too."

"Ugh. And you wonder why I'm not interested in a husband," Margaret laughed.

"You'd never consider anyone like that. He's too far below your class. You'd marry a rich and refined gentleman," Ruth said.

"Really? For a small-town girl, Ruth, sometimes you surprise me," she said, chewing a bit from her sandwich. "I'm crazy enough to marry anyone for love. Class or no class, rich or poor, it wouldn't matter. But right now, I'm having too much fun on my own, dependent on no one." Margaret pushed her naturally red hair away from her face.

Ruth got quiet. She put down her sandwich and took a sip of coffee.

"You're not eating. What gives? Something is bothering you. Tell me, please," Margaret said, touching Ruth's hand briefly before digging back into her sandwich.

Ruth sipped more coffee. "Yes, well." She hesitated. Margaret waited quietly until she was ready to go on. "I've been caring for a cancer case that's been tough. The lady has uterine cancer like my mother died from and the treatments are still brutal and ineffective. I hate to see how much pain she's going through with those radiation treatments." Ruth teared up and Margaret patted her hand.

"She told the nurses I'm the only one who treats her decent. She was hysteric with pain at the time, but it caused a stir, as you can imagine. Now, some of them look at me funny and I hear remarks behind my back," Ruth said, taking an embroidered linen handkerchief from her purse and dabbing her eyes.

"Oh, they're just jealous of your nursing ability."

"It's more than that. The lady is Black. Some of them refuse to care for her. You know, they have their ideas. To make matters worse, the doctor is Jewish, and they say horrible things about him, too. They talk like Nazis," Ruth said, dropping her voice lower, causing Margaret to lean in to hear her.

"Oh, I see," Margaret said. "Makes you wonder why we fought that damn war. You know, I grew up with this crap. My parents saved all those horrible pro-Nazi *Dearborn Independent* newspapers Ford published in the 1920s. They even keep a framed photo of Hitler giving Ford a medal in 1938. It makes me sick. It's no wonder I can't live here anymore."

"They're your family, though," Ruth replied, taking a bite of sandwich.

Margaret nodded, a grimace on her face. "Anyway, forget about me. What are you going to do? Can you handle it?"

Straightening up in her seat, Ruth said, "I can take their meanness most days, but I won't stay here long even though I like the work."

"What about your patient?"

"Oh, I'll see that through. The worst part is knowing the lady will die soon like my mother did. I find that hard to take sometimes. It brings up memories of standing by her hospital bed as she lay dying. I didn't even hold her hand, I was so confused and afraid," Ruth said, crying.

"Ruthie, now stop that. You were just a kid. Death is scary, even for those of us who have seen so much of it," Margaret said. "What's your patient's name?"

"Ruby," Ruth answered, brightening a little.

"Just take care of Ruby as best you can and then get the hell out of here and go back to your beloved U.P.," Margaret said, trying to make a joke.

"I think that's what I need."

SEPTEMBER 1946

Ruby died the next month in the middle of the night when Ruth was on duty. Her family, who had been holding a vigil, stood quietly by her bedside in a private room that the gynecologist, Dr. Jacobson, insisted she have over the objections and complaints of the head nurse. Only Ruth knew that the doctor had covered the extra cost of the room.

After Ruby died, the duty nurse came over to Ruth to tell her to "get those people out so we can remove the body and clean the room. You seem to know how to talk to their kind. Get them out of there."

When Ruth entered the room, Dr. Jacobson was consoling Ruby's father. "Arthur, I'm sorry I couldn't do more for her," he said, resting his hand on Arthur's shoulder as a comfort.

When he saw Ruth, Dr. Jacobson said, "Please come over here. I think you've seen them but let me introduce you. this is Ruby's father, Arthur, and her sister, Anne. Arthur, Ruth cared for your daughter these last months."

"Oh, yes, we are so grateful for your care. You treated my little girl kindly," Arthur offered. He towered above Ruth and bent down slightly to hold both her hands in his, shocking Ruth with his boldness to hold a white woman's hands.

"You served as an Army nurse in the Philippines, right?" Arthur asked, looking into Ruth's eyes. "Ruby told me. She liked you. Thank you for treating her right. I'll bet she didn't tell you she also was a nurse in the Army." This surprised Ruth, and she began to relax.

"No, she never mentioned that to me," Ruth said, wondering why it had never come up in their conversations.

Still holding Ruth's hands, Arthur said, "They made her care for German prisoners. Hardcore Nazis they were. Nasty. She didn't talk about her work, but I could tell she didn't like it. She was only in for a few months toward the end of the war when she got this here cancer. I'll wonder to my dying day if she got sick because of those Nazis, but Doctor Jacobson told me not to think like that. He's a good man. Better than most men you'll meet." Arthur sighed in pain, releasing his grip on Ruth's hands to take a handkerchief out of his coat pocket to dry his eyes.

"The Good Lord must have needed a nurse, because he's taken her home with him," Arthur said confidently, tears streamed down his face.

"Amen," Anne said, standing over looking at Ruby. "He has taken away your pain, Little Sister." She smiled sadly.

NOVEMBER 1946

Ruth set a brisk pace walking from her sister Linda's house on Maple Street over to Portage Avenue. She left the house quietly at 5:30 a.m., taking the shopping list Linda had left on the table for Ruth to pick up from the Red Owl grocery store when she returned in the afternoon. The back of her ankles chaffed from her new boots riding up and down, and she made a mental note to wear a pair of wool socks inside her boots tomorrow. She hoped her nylons would make it through without any runs, but she kept a fresh pair in her locker for emergencies, if they did.

Ruth had moved up to Sault Ste. Marie and started work-ing at the War Memorial Hospital in October, so she knew the walk took her about thirty minutes in good weather. With an early snowfall last night, she allowed more time. She also planned to stop at the café, which opened at 6 a.m., for break-fast before clocking in at the hospital.

As she walked through the snow, Ruth thought, *I'm always behind. All the good men are taken, I'm sure. Maybe I should go back to Detroit. There are plenty of jobs and the pay is better. The work wasn't like the war, but it was challenging. Here nothing seems to happen.*

Older than Big Bay or Marquette, the Soo, as locals called it, dated from 1668 when the French established a settlement. Ruth had learned that Portage Avenue took its name from the days when men and horse teams hauled ships around the rapids separating Lake Superior from the St. Mary's River before the first of the Soo Locks were begun over a hundred years earlier. As she rushed by an old bar her sister said had been a speakeasy during Prohibition, Ruth looked across the street at the large factory that blocked Ruth's view of the river. She cursed her timing as she saw a cloud of ash belch out from the chimney, covering the white snow. Ruth longed to get out of town where the air was clean, but she knew that would be months away.

Ruth loved the feel of snowflakes on her face, but the biting air caused her to pull up her hand-knitted wool scarf covering her mouth and nose and adjusted her matching hat. Crossing the canal bridge, she left the factory behind her. The air smelled fresher as the snow crunched under her boots.

Below freezing by the sound of the crackle, Ruth thought.

When Ruth reached the corner of Ashmun and Portage, where Archie's cab company hugged the corner, she waved to him and he yelled, "Hey, Ruth, where are you going in this weather? Fancy a ride? Give you one for free."

Archie had lost his leg in Italy, so he qualified for a car under a government program that helped him set up his cab business.

"No thanks, Archie. Maybe some other time. I'm just going up here to the café for breakfast," she said, pointing ahead.

"You're one tough Swede," Archie declared. "We Italians like to ride whenever we get a chance." He let out a laugh.

Ruth realized how comfortable she felt with veterans like Archie, and that new patient, John Solonen, who had come into the hospital a few days ago. *People like Linda*, Ruth thought, *could never understand my service.* Her sister seemed both appalled and envious, but only asked Ruth questions about dances and glimpses of MacArthur. Most people were like that. They would rather fantasize about war than ask or listen.

Combat veterans are different, Ruth thought thinking of John—a big kid who survived hell as an aerial gunner in Europe. He had an easy laugh, beautiful smile, endless jokes, and wry observations like an old wise man.

Leaving Archie behind, she crossed the street toward Tony's Café, a narrow restaurant squeezed in between the bars along Portage Avenue.

"Hey, Ruth," Tony called out when she pushed through the door, trying to keep out the snow rushing in behind her. "Great weather we're having, eh?"

He said that everyday rain, shine, snow, or sleet and she knew the proper reply, "It sure is, Tony. You got any coffee and eggs today?"

A quick study, Tony had remembered her name since the first time she walked through the door in October. Inquisitive and a good listener despite his talkative nature, they quickly determined they were both veterans. He served in Italy and Germany as a radio operator. Grazed in the arm on patrol, Tony recovered in a field hospital and appreciated Ruth's service as a war nurse. Ruth liked to stop at Tony's place coming or going from work to get a dose of his friendly optimism, which she needed today as she worried she had made a mistake coming to the Soo.

Tony quickly delivered her food to the booth Ruth always sat in, back away from the door. "I added a piece of French toast today," Tony said with a smile, knowing Ruth loved it. "How's business?" he asked.

"Slow," she answered.

"I heard about that guy who blew his eye out a few days ago. Poor bastard. I know his dad, a Finn from the old country. His son, John, I think, served as a gunner with the 20th out of England. Gunner. Man, that was no picnic in the underbelly of those planes. Anyway, his old man said John nearly had his ass blown off more than once and had to bail out twice. You know, Ernie Pyle even interviewed him—I heard it on the radio! They also wrote it up in the *Detroit Free Press*. Jeez. Poor bastard spends four years fighting the damn Krauts without a scratch. Then he comes back home and loses his eye to an exploding bottle of O-SO Grape soda. Go figure. What the hell kind of work can he get now?"

"I don't know," Ruth said. She had not thought about what John could do with one eye and no high school diploma in this town, but he had such a lovely smile and that rakish head of blond hair he combed back like a movie star made her believe he would be all right. Plus, he made her laugh.

After she clocked in at the hospital, Ruth went straight to John's room to see if he was still there. He was up eating his breakfast.

"You're a sight for sore eyes," he laughed. "At least this one that I can see you with." His pearly smile spread across his face. Ruth realized how much she loved to see him smile.

She laughed. "Glad you're in good spirits. Have you been giving the nurses a hard time?"

"Sure, it's fun to give you nurses trouble," John said laughing, "but when do you think they'll let me out of here?"

"We'll see what the doctor says. Dr. Hatala should be coming soon on his rounds."

"Hatala's a good man. He has to be; he's a Finn, like me," John laughed. "He served, too, so I trust him."

CHAPTER 9

WHITE GAUZE

(DECEMBER 1946)

———

After receiving multiple Christmas cards and letters, Ruth envied the exciting post-war lives of her Army friends. After Alice returned to California, she married a childhood sweetheart and was now expecting her first child. Margaret had made it to occupied Japan, and Esther finagled an assignment to Salzburg and hoped to transfer to Berlin next year. Reading about their adventures made Ruth regret moving north to this manufacturing town, but she felt trapped by a promise to Linda to help her out until Stewart returned home from the West Coast, where he remained in uniform after the war. The town, which had boomed during the war with defense production at the tannery and carbide factory, now spiraled in decline as production adjusted to post-war realities.

To Ruth, the town felt like a balloon slowly deflating as opportunities spirited away. *They will always need the hospital, at least*, Ruth thought.

The loud complaints of a customer caught Ruth's attention as she sat drinking coffee.

"Damn. I wish that war had kept going," he said. "We all did so well here. Plenty of work for everyone. Even the girls had work. I was getting somewhere, eh? Even bought good hunting land near Hessel. Just laid the foundation for the camp. How will I afford to finish it when they cut my job at the tannery?"

"That's a shame all right. But at least you own the land and you have a place to go outside of town. You can start with a tent," Tony said, giving a wink to Ruth sitting in the booth behind the man.

"A tent!" the customer scoffed. "What a foolish idea. Who wants to stay in a tent? Then there's the damn taxes. A man can't get a break."

Ruth stared into her coffee, angrily calculating how many dead and maimed soldiers it took to buy this man's hunting land. But she also ached knowing the end of the war ended her opportunities, too. She still stung from a conversation with a loan manager at the bank a few days earlier when she inquired about a GI loan for a house.

You're not from around here, are you? Yes, I see you have your paperwork in order showing you served. An Army nurse, eh? Only a year? I see. Oh, in the Philippines. That must have been a nice assignment in the tropics, like Hawaii no doubt. Lucky you. Well, that's very nice, and if you come back with your husband, or perhaps a male relative who can co-sign, we might be able to make arrangements. Of course, you would need to put down a major portion of the cost. Anyway, for now, we can't support your request. Good day.

The phrases of rejection spun around her mind, making her angrier and angrier, as she waited for Wilma to join her.

She held her coffee cup tightly in both hands. *I wish I could smash it on that smug bastard's head*, Ruth thought, recalling the face of the young man at the bank.

"Ruth? Are you all right?" Tony asked.

Looking up, she saw the customer had left, muttering to himself as he walked out the café door, probably headed to the bar next door. "Oh. I'm fine," Ruth lied.

"You look like you'd like to hit someone with that cup. How 'bout I fill it up instead?" Tony laughed softly, seeming to study her, assessing what she might do next.

"Sure," Ruth replied as she caught sight of Wilma entering the café and waved to her. As she sat down across from Ruth, Tony said, "I know you Navy types prefer rot gut coffee, but all I can serve you is the best cup of coffee you'll ever get in this town."

Wilma laughed. "I guess that will have to do, Tony."

After Tony poured her coffee and went back behind the counter that ran along one side of the café opposite the booths, Wilma said, "Ruth, are you doing all right? I haven't heard from you since you talked to the bank. How bad was it?"

"That brat told me to bring a man and a lot of cash the next time I try to get a loan. It makes me so mad. We served just like all these bastards did guarding the locks and going home to their mothers at night. The Philippines was no tropical vacation! We earned our benefits." Ruth raised her voice, knowing Tony had heard every word, but pretended to be absorbed in sorting silverware. "We saved lives," Ruth added.

"What are you going to do?" Wilma asked.

"Leave. I don't belong here. Maybe I should go back home to Big Bay. Marquette has a hospital. I could work there again like I did during nursing training."

"I don't think it will be any different in Marquette. I would hate to see you leave because I'd be on my own again, but I understand if you do go. I was born here, so I'm sort of use to this place, but one thing I've learned since I came back from the war is to keep my mouth shut and keep to myself. I came back for my elderly parents, but I'll probably stay after they're gone. This place grows on you if you give it a chance," Wilma said. "So, bide your time on the house."

"That guy at the bank shook me up. It hurt listening to him demean me and my service."

"I've known that kid at the bank since he wore diapers. He was bad then and he's worse now. Try another bank or one outside of town—maybe a co-op. The way I handle people like him is I smile and laugh at the appropriate times like the southern belles who came up here with their husbands for work, but I pay them no mind. We both have looked death straight in the eye. We know what's important and we know who we are. And there are good people here. You'll meet them, but you have to give it a chance."

I wonder if I really do know who I am, Ruth thought later, as she watched snow falling outside the car window as Wilma gave her a ride home. *And I don't know if I really belong here. Granted, the town has its charms. The hospital is good. The old red stone architecture downtown reminds me of Marquette.*

"Here you go, Ruth," Wilma said, pulling up in front of Linda's house.

"Would you like to come in?" Ruth asked.

"No, thank you. Your sister is a lovely woman, but I think she doesn't like me. You know my motto: keep my mouth shut, but the corollary is to avoid situations where my big mouth will get me in trouble," she laughed. "I'll pick you up tomorrow. You won't want to walk in this mess."

As Ruth pushed her way through the snowed-in sidewalk, she recalled the first months after she'd arrived in September. Ruth found it fun to be with her sister and she loved reading to Nora and playing with her when Linda had a headache or felt too tired. Ruth also loved taking the ferry over to the town's twin city, Sault Ste. Marie, Ontario, Canada for the day. She and Linda, wearing their best clothes, went to window shop, dine, and go to the movie theater. Ruth began a collection of fine English teacups, bright spots she would enjoy no matter where she might live.

But Ruth understood why Wilma felt Linda did not like her, because Linda told her as much. "She's mannish and fat. I don't know how she served as a nurse on a hospital ship."

Now, as Ruth came into the house, Nora ran toward her laughing, a book in her hand. *She's such a happy child. She looks like an angel*, Ruth thought grabbing her up into her arms before taking off her boots and coat.

"Book! Book!" Nora cried, meaning she wanted Ruth to scoop her up into her lap to read to her.

"Just a minute, Nora. Let me get my coat and boots off. Where's Mama?" she asked, and Nora pointed back to the kitchen making a face. "Let me check on her. You go sit down and I'll read to you soon, okay?"

Nora laughed, running over to their reading chair, repeating, "Okay, okay."

Ruth and Linda were opposites. They disagreed on almost everything. Ruth liked to read; Linda liked to shop. Ruth liked to wear sensible clothes, even pants. Linda liked frilly, impractical clothes unsuitable for outings at the shore or in the woods. Ruth had attended college and traveled in the Army, expanding her world. She had seen different people in the cities and overseas. She knew there was more to the world. Linda had married at seventeen. She had little interest in Ruth or anything she valued. She seemed to hate that Ruth became a nurse and served during the war.

As Ruth walked into the kitchen, she noticed a letter on the table. Linda appeared to have been crying and throwing pots around. A dish lay in pieces on the floor. Ruth noticed with relief it was a cheap plate, not the English china.

When Linda saw her, she yelled, screaming, "You were spoiled. Anna sent you to nursing school. You never could have gone on your own. You were too dumb in school. I had nothing. She did nothing for me!" She broke down sobbing.

Ruth stood studying Linda and wondering how to reply. She had learned long ago that if she responded in kind it would lead to a long, bitter argument that would take days to recover from. By now, Linda's hurtful remarks did not always cause pain. Ruth felt numb to her common taunts. Linda's periodic outbursts had erupted unexpectedly for as long as Ruth could remember. The first time she saw Linda on the floor kicking and screaming, she rushed to ask their mother, *What's wrong with Linda? Is she sick?* Their mother replied, *Nothing, let her be until she calms down.*

If anyone was spoiled, Ruth thought now, *it is you, Linda. Ma spoiled you by indulging you. She even bought you your own special soap, when the family barely scraped together enough to eat, and it often meant Ma went without the little we did have.* Anna had explained to Ruth that their mother felt a special bond with Linda, the beautiful twin that survived. Later, Anna believed, their mother felt a bottomless guilt over the abuse she could not stop and the damage it caused. Ruth felt sad thinking about the past, wanting to comfort Linda, but she realized this outburst had nothing to do with herself or Anna. Something had happened and Ruth suspected whatever it was lay in that letter.

"Are you all right, Linda?" Ruth asked, ignoring Linda's hurtful comments. "Has something happened?"

"I…I…Stewart says he's not coming back. He says he's found someone else." Linda shook with anger. "How could he abandon me?"

Ruth did not feel surprised. A handsome man, Stewart had attracted female attention since high school. Ruth had suspected another woman when Stewart delayed coming home to his family. Liaisons happened so often during the war. Ruth reddened, thinking of her own dalliance with Rich. She worried what this news would mean for Linda and Nora.

"He says he wants a divorce," Linda said icily, "but I just called him to tell him I will never give him a divorce to marry some whore. And I told him I will make sure he never sees his daughter again."

When Stewart called Linda back an hour later as Ruth read a story to Nora, Ruth saw Linda listen then hang up after she said, "Yes."

"He says he's working to get to get a transfer to the Coast Guard station. He hopes to be back by the summer. He asked if I could forgive him," Linda relayed, a satisfied expression on her face. Ruth wondered if Linda ever would forgive Stewart, but she admired Linda's determination to keep her family together.

The following week, Ruth again had a morning shift. She missed talking with John who had been released a few days earlier. She walked onto the second floor when she heard Dr. Hatala.

"Miss Amundsen, you're here!" the doctor called out, sounding relieved. His voice was muffled by the cloth mask across his face.

"I need you to put on a mask and gown. I need your help. Quickly, please."

When Ruth returned, Dr. Hatala was waiting outside the room. "It's bad. Two kids were burned in a car accident out near Bay Mills. I've called Miss Walsh in, too. I know you both had a lot of experience with burn patients during the war."

Ruth's heart raced. Children. She felt nauseous and her hands began to shake. She had avoided working pediatrics since she began nursing training at St. Luke's Hospital in 1939, realizing seeing children in pain or watching them die overwhelmed her. She had not been able to stop crying when they could not save that Filipino boy who was crushed by an Army truck in Batangas. *I don't know what I would have done if Wilson hadn't been there to help me,* she thought.

But a lot had happened since training and those early days in the Philippines, and she understood the nightmare of a burned child for the family. She felt herself settle into a professional demeanor, as she saw the doctor seemed nervous. *We can't both be hysterical,* Ruth thought.

"Let me see them," Ruth said, feeling calm. The room held two hospital beds, one on each side of the room. Each bed held the small body of a burned child. Mrs. Baker and a nurse Ruth did not recognize stood by one bed waiting. They appeared to have been assisting the doctor as he cut the burned clothes away from one of the children. Ruth thought they both looked lost about what to do.

"Amundsen," he said dropping formalities, "cut the clothes away from the other child." Ruth grabbed a scissor from a tray and walked over to the second bed.

Mrs. Baker, who enjoyed her status as head nurse, usually worked at her desk. She could have served in the war as a nurse, but chose to stay in the Soo, looking to marry an eligible doctor. She failed to find a doctor and seemed to detest women veterans. Even through her mask, Ruth could tell she shot her an ugly look, perhaps thinking she should be the one to take charge of the other child.

Wilma Walsh stormed into the room wearing a mask and gown.

"Walsh, please help Amundsen remove the burned clothes."

"Were you Army, too, Wilma?" Mrs. Baker asked, sounding condescending.

"No. I served in the Navy at Pearl Harbor, then on a hospital ship," Wilma said, her attention fixed on the child.

"I had no idea," Baker said.

"You never asked," Wilma replied.

A small form almost identical to the one the doctor worked on lay on the white bed, covered in a confusing tangle of singed red wool over what looked like a dark blue flannel dress. Handmade wool mittens, matching hat, and stockings completed the outfit.

"Sunday best," Wilma said.

"Made with love and care," Ruth added sadly.

As Wilma and Ruth swept their eyes over their patient, assessing her condition, they both realized she was Ojibwe. "No wonder Baker is in such a bad temper," Wilma whispered to Ruth.

The smell of charred, wet wool rose off the body. It mingled with other smells that Ruth recognized as burned hair and skin. She and Wilma exchanged a quick look of controlled terror. Wilma wiped a tear away with the back of her hand. Ruth steeled herself for the work ahead thinking, *I've seen much worse burn cases in Manila. Stay calm*, to reassure herself.

Ruth worked like a possessed person to clear away the burned clothes with quick and delicate moves, cutting away the large pieces that did not cling to the skin first and then working down toward the skin. Checking the blood pressure as she worked, she remembered the burns of the Japanese prisoner the troops had captured near Batangas. At first, she saw an enemy, but after Wilson ordered her to treat him as her patient, she saw a man, filled with fear, shame, pain, and gratitude as she had cleaned out the gangrene and treated his burns.

"Amundsen! How does it look?" Dr. Hatala asked.

Finishing talking her vitals, Ruth said, "Her blood pressure is elevated, but she's stable. The heavy wool coat protected her, but her hands and legs are bad."

"Same here. These heavy winter clothes may have saved them. What about her face and head?"

Ruth studied her face, beautiful and delicate, despite a coating of dark soot. A heavy wool hat covered the top of her head. Two braids spilled out below the hat, where one lay burned against her cheek.

"One side of her face is burned. The top of her head seems okay, but I can't be sure until we remove everything and clean her up."

Once they cut away the clothes, the doctor checked for the dead tissue to remove, and then Wilma and Ruth worked together to dress the wounds. Dr. Hatala admiringly watched, occasionally making suggestions. He even allowed them to put in the intravenous drips. When they finished, the two little girls looked like two identical mummies. Dr. Hatala said, "Now the real work begins."

Ruth knew the first hours and days of care determined the possibility of recovery. "Doctor," Ruth said, "preventing infection and keeping them hydrated are what we prioritized in the Philippines. But I've seen burn victims who seemed to be on the mend, only to die. Their pain is so dreadful some seem to give up."

"Yes, yes," Doctor Hatala replied as if he were speaking to a colleague. "Carefully monitor their fluid intake and the outtake to make sure they are balanced and there is no internal bleeding that could kill them. Do you have any suggestions?"

"I think Wilma and I should focus on their care, alternating twelve hours on and twelve hours off until we know they are stable. We can train a couple of the new nurses how to care for burn victims. They can help. Also, it may sound strange, but I've seen it make a difference with soldiers. The girls' names are Joyce and Joan. If we say their names, they know we care and are helping to bring them back."

Mrs. Baker objected to "wasting" extra resources on the girls, plus the other three family members recovering in another ward, but Dr. Hatala overruled her.

Throughout each shift, the nurses frequently monitored their IV drips and moistened their lips. They checked how much they drank and their outtake, which they collected and measured. Dr. Hatala looked for clues of their internal condition and removed dead tissue to encourage healing. Ruth talked to the girls and encouraged others on the team to do the same.

"It helps the sickest patients stay connected to life. They can hear voices reassure them and it can help distract them from pain and discomfort," Ruth told a young nurse who had overheard her talking to the girls about the weather, as well as stories of skiing, snowshoeing, and skating. "You know, Wilma has a running discussion with them on the merits of the Tigers' baseball record and hockey teams and players," Ruth told her, "Maybe talk about cooking, knitting, or something else you're interested in."

The second week was much like the first week. Joyce and Joan opened their eyes more often, although they were not fully alert. They seemed in more pain as they healed. Not to hurt them more than necessary was paramount. Wilma showed Ruth a technique she had learned for changing the dressing that caused less distress. The nurses all marveled at the strength and stoicism of the girls: no crying, just an involuntary jerk or small noise occasionally.

Joyce reminded Ruth of her niece, which at first horrified her as she dreamed of Nora being on fire, but as Joyce got a little better, it made her feel happy. Joan seemed to grow stronger quicker. She had been removed from the burning vehicle before Joyce and suffered less injury. Ruth felt joy watching both girls heal.

After one month, the girls were strong enough for Dr. Hatala, a skilled cosmetic surgeon, to begin skin grafting. They seemed out of the woods and Wilma and Ruth returned to regular shifts.

One day as Ruth walked through the halls on her way to her ward, she saw Joe walking toward her looking relieved, but tired.

"Joe, I can't believe it's you. How are you? Do you live in the Soo?" Ruth said.

"No, I am living near Brimley," Joe said. He did not seem surprised to see Ruth. He acted like it was perfectly normal to see Ruth in Manila one day and in the Soo the next, even though it had been over a year since they'd seen each other. "You've been caring for my nieces. They were in that accident."

"I had no idea. I never saw you here," Ruth said.

"No, they wouldn't let us see them because they worried about infection, but I could tell they received good care. Dr. Hatala is a fine man. He treated them well. When he told me you and a former Navy nurse were caring for the girls, I knew it would be all right," he said. Then added, "I'm glad you were here for them. Dr. Hatala said you saved their lives. They would not have made it without you." Joe looked so directly into Ruth's eyes that she blushed, embarrassed.

CHAPTER 10

TWO WINTERS A YEAR

(WINTER 1946 AND 1947)

———

"Will this snow ever end? They need to plow these streets," Wilma yelled loudly, as she waved a thank you to some boys who pushed her car free of deep snow that trapped her after she picked up Ruth. "I can't believe it. We finish one year with winter and we start a new year with more of it." Wilma muttered, wiping the inside of the car window with a mitten, a vain attempt to clear the fog. "This window never wants to clear."

Ruth noticed locals, like Wilma, cursed the winter, seemingly surprised by its arrival each year, but were well adapted to its fury nonetheless. Ruth watched her breath cloud as she spoke, "That's two winters a year. That's what we used to say up in Big Bay."

"That's right. We spend half the damn year in winter, no matter which way you figure it. Man, my feet are freezing. This car's heater is useless," Wilma complained.

"It'll warm up by the time we reach the hospital," Ruth laughed. Wilma shot her a look and broke out laughing.

"Ain't that the truth? Maybe we should joy ride up and down Ashmun to help it warm up. It's pretty quiet with everyone on holiday," Wilma laughed.

They volunteered to work extra hours between Christmas and New Year's so others could spend time with their families and found themselves on the same shift but different floors. Ruth loved that winter had started so early this year, making up for her hot and humid Christmas in the Philippines last year. But as wave after wave of snow piled up in town and the windchill off Lake Superior increased, she wondered how she would feel later in January, or February, or March, or later, if she lasted that long once Linda's husband returned home.

Ruth's frequent walks downtown to window shop and on to the hospital had declined in early December as heavy snows filled in the sidewalks. She took Wilma up on regular rides to and from work when their shifts coincided and relied on Archie's cab the rest of the time, including picking her up from the Red Owl, arms filled with paper bags of food to take home.

"Have you heard anything from John?" Wilma asked. Everyone seemed to know everyone in this town, and Wilma was no exception. Wilma knew his sister, Louise, and heard stories of his wartime service. Ruth had an impression she liked him.

Ruth shook her head. Over a month had passed since John left the hospital and Ruth heard nothing from him. "Don't worry. He'll turn up, and if he doesn't, there are plenty of fish in the sea, especially if you go back to Detroit or some other city," Wilma said.

The parking lot looked like a white field of snow, but Wilma found a relatively clear spot a night shift worker had just left. "This is good. We'll worry about getting out later," Wilma said, before adding, "We may be shoveling ourselves out if the plow comes through and blocks us in. Good thing I have a shovel in the trunk. We can take turns. I also have sand. You have to be prepared for anything."

Later, during morning visiting hours, Ruth sat at the nurse's station updating charts after making her rounds. She thought about what Wilma had said about John. Then, when she looked up and saw him standing at the high counter in front of her, she worried that Wilma had called Louise who told John to come to see her. She hoped he had come in on his own.

"Hey," he said with an awkward mix of bravado and shyness. "What do you think about my new eye?"

Ruth remembered John's remaining hazel eye changed from brown to blue to green to gray, depending on the background. She saw his new eye, made of glass, had multiple flecks of color in it to match his real eye as it changed, an important detail that Ruth hoped made John feel whole again.

"It looks great," Ruth said. "Very natural."

John smiled broadly. "Yeah, the doc did a good job, eh?"

Ruth smiled hearing the familiar lilting "eh" that ended John's sentences, an accent she had missed hearing when she lived outside the U.P. Abruptly, John said, "Hey, what about that date?"

"You do know it's twenty below zero outside. A little cold for a motorcycle ride, don't you think?" Ruth replied laughing.

"No, not that. I have a ride down to Rudyard to meet up with my cousins to go to their cabin in Cedarville. They have a nice place with a sauna. Good people. I think you would like them. Say, you do know how to dress warm, don't you?" John said.

"Of course, I do. I'm from Big Bay," replied Ruth.

"What about snowshoeing?" John asked.

"I don't have a pair here, but I enjoy it," Ruth said.

"I have an extra pair. We snowshoe into the cabin this time of year and might need them to get out to their fish shack, depending on the snow. Have you ever gone ice fishing?" John asked with a smirk, seeming to hope she had no idea what she might be getting into.

"Not lately," Ruth answered, having ice fished with Eddie and Mary in their shanty. "I'm off this Saturday." As she spoke, she thought through her wardrobe and wondered if her new boots would work on the ice.

"Are you off Sunday, too?" John asked. "It's a long drive down to the cabin in this weather and it would be better if we overnighted. My cousins have plenty of room."

"What are you getting at? What do you take me for?" Ruth stood up and put her hands on her hips. Ruth wondered if all Finns moved this fast.

"Oh, no. Nothing like that. I didn't mean anything bad," John said looking less than angelic, as if he would be game for whatever Ruth would agree to, but he added, "My cousin, Elias, and his wife, Leena, will be there. And Leena would beat the hell out of me if I did anything wrong." John laughed.

His sincerity and humor disarmed Ruth and before she could stop herself, she'd said, yes, knowing Linda would be angry she would not walk with her to church on Sunday.

"Okay, then. I'll pick you up this Saturday at 6 a.m. Can you handle that?" John teased.

"Oh, I think I can handle that," she said, nodding her head and wondering what she had just agreed to.

After work when Ruth told Linda she intended to spend the weekend at a cabin in Cedarville, she burst into a rant against the idea that would last the rest of the week.

"What do you mean you are going to spend the weekend with a strange man? You'll ruin your reputation in town. And mine! What will people think if I let my little sister run off into the woods? You have never been the same since you lived in that apartment in Detroit and went halfway across the world unchaperoned in the Army." Linda railed.

Nora looked anxious hearing her mother raise her voice, so Ruth made a silly face to reassure her.

"It's dirty of him to ask you to stay overnight on your first date. I am sure he must be no good. Where does he work, anyway?" she nagged.

Wilma laughed when Ruth shared highlights of Linda's assault at lunch.

"Goodness. Does she think any girl who lives in an apartment must be a whore?" she said, lowering her voice. "That's a good one. And doesn't she know we did have chaperones during the war: first there was Uncle Sam and then there was the head nurse, who watched us like a hawk. At least I know mine did." Wilma laughed.

"It's not that funny," Ruth replied, trying to not to laugh.

"Did you tell her to go to hell? And what's with this 'little sister' business, anyway? You're a grown woman. And a veteran for goodness sake," Wilma said.

"No, it's no use arguing with her. I just let her complain and now and again I say things like 'really,' 'you don't say,' or 'goodness.' It drives her nuts," Ruth said to Wilma, who looked dumfounded until she burst out laughing, drawing stares from other nurses eating in the cafeteria.

"I had no idea how devilish you could be," Wilma said after she regained control.

Linda carried on relentlessly each day that week before Ruth went to work and after she came home. Her ranting reminded Ruth of that doctor in Batangas just before they took him away in a straitjacket, but it did not stop her from going to Cedarville.

When Saturday came, Ruth felt relieved to get out of the house, although she wished she could bring Nora with her. But, she knew, Linda would never allow that. Ruth planned to tell her stories of her adventures on the ice and snow when she returned.

John arrived early, but Ruth was ready. A hunting buddy whose name Ruth did not catch drove them to Rudyard, thirty miles south of the Soo. Darkness shrouded the landscape as they drove on US 2, the headlights creating narrow bands of light through lightly falling snow. Having arrived in town by train from the west, Ruth felt excitement to be heading toward the Straits of Mackinac, where Lake Michigan and Lake Huron meet. Ruth saw glimpses of rolling farmland and wooded stands of green spruce and pine captured in the headlights through the falling snow. She was glad she wasn't the one driving in this weather.

John sat in the front, talking to the diver in a mixture of English and Finnish, making it hard to follow their conversation. Ruth sat in the back with their gear. Linda's warnings and opinions began to seep into her thoughts as she realized she was alone in a car in the middle of nowhere with two strange men, but somehow, she felt safe and secure. She opened her coat to cool off in the heated car, even though her feet felt cold. As the car glided over the snow packed road, she drifted asleep.

She woke up when they stopped in front of a one story, boxy house. Its porch light and living room lights were shining in the darkness.

"Here we are," John said as he shook hands with his friend and held the seat open for Ruth to climb out, then grabbed the bags from the seat. "Go on ahead. That's Elias waiting at the door." John waved and yelled, "This is Ruth."

Ruth stepped out into the fresh air that seemed even colder after the smoky, hot car. As she walked up to the door, John followed close behind her as the car pulled away. He dropped their bags on the small open porch, which had been freshly swept clean of snow. Then he went back to retrieve two pair of handmade snowshoes sticking into the snowbank.

Elias greeted Ruth and John at the door with a friendly face. He wore a red-and-black checkered wool shirt and heavy wool pants, looking ready for anything the U.P. cold could throw at him, except he only wore slippers—no boots.

Ruth felt happy to see Leena standing inside behind Elias. She had a kind and sympathetic smile. Instead of the dress and skirts, Ruth noticed that most women wore in town, Leena wore a stylish ski outfit with warm pants and a bright, red-and-white wool sweater.

"Hey, Cousin," Elias said hitting John on the shoulder. He gestured for Ruth to enter ahead of them, an unusual show of chivalry. "You must be Ruth. I'm Elias and this is my wife, Leena," he said, shaking her hand.

"Come on in," Leena said, taking charge. "John, leave those snowshoes on the porch. No one's going to steal them at this hour. Elias, bring those bags in here so they will stay warm. Ruth, you can throw your coat on the davenport. Take your boots off by the door. John, knock that snow off your boots before you come in."

Handing Ruth a pair of slippers, Leena said, "Here, Ruth, put these on to keep your feet dry."

Ruth did a quick survey of what looked like a one-bedroom house with a kitchen that opened into the dining and living room. Ruth wondered if Elias had built the warm and cozy house. Flowery wallpaper appeared to be the main decoration, with a few photos on an end table, and magazines stacked neatly on the coffee table. Ruth saw no books.

"Where are my slippers?" John asked removing his boots.

"You scamp. I know you wouldn't wear slippers if I had them for you. Sit down, drink some coffee, and behave," Leena directed.

"Now, you sit down here, Ruth," Leena continued, pointing to a seat at a table bursting with a breakfast of pancakes, eggs, and a plate piled with strips of bacon. "You must be famished. We need to eat a good breakfast before we set off for the camp because we won't eat again until supper time. The boys have a lot of work to do to set up the sauna and check on the fish shack."

Ruth obediently sat down at the table. Leena automatically placed a cup of coffee in front of her. "You take cream and sugar?" Leena asked.

"No, she likes it black with no sugar," John interjected, surprising Ruth that he knew.

Maybe he had talked to Tony at the café, she wondered. Small towns, she knew, did not keep secrets.

"But I'll take some of that fresh cream and maybe a little sugar," John said to Leena, holding up his cup.

"Oh, you. You can help yourself, John. I'm not your waitress. There's fresh cream in the icebox. Fend for yourself," she said, gently batting John with a wooden spoon.

Ruth felt herself relax into the warmth and casual kindness she felt.

"John tells us you're Swedish from Big Bay, right? You know, our family is Finnish, but we hold no grudges against the Swedes for occupying Finland. We reserve that for the Russians for stealing Karelia," Elias said with a smirk.

Ruth realized she would need to visit the Carnegie Library in town to study Swedish and Finnish history to keep up with the banter in the future. "Yes," she said, "I'm half Swedish from my mother's side, but my last name, Amundsen, is Danish. I even have some Irish and Dutch blood, so I guess you could say I'm a mutt." Ruth surprised them with her self-effacing frankness. They laughed, enjoying the joke with her.

"Well," said Leena, "a lot of the families here in Rudyard claim to be a hundred percent Finnish, but we have our own mixing. My family, for example, is Norwegian and Finnish. The pure Finns tend to live in the Copper Country, as you may know. That is where John was born. In Mohawk, he may have told you. You cannot throw a rock in any direction without hitting a Finn up there."

"I haven't had a chance to tell her anything," John said. "But you are telling her everything anyway."

"We want her to know what she's getting into, you rogue," Leena said.

"Oh, you two, leave the gal alone. They're just teasing. Pay them no mind, Ruth," Elias interjected. "Listen, around this part of the country there's a mix of French Canadians, Italians, Germans, and the Ojibwe people: you get the picture. There are also a lot of Finns, farmers mostly, on Sugar Island, including one of John's sisters. And truth be told, although none of these hardheaded Finns would ever admit it, our grandmother was part Swedish. Do you speak Swedish?"

"No," Ruth answered. "I knew some Swedish as a child, but my mother died young, and I couldn't keep it up. My mother's step-family spoke Swedish, but we lost contact with them after she died." Ruth surprised herself that she shared that information. She usually did not talk about her family with strangers. "I think my mother wanted us to learn English so we could get along here."

"You'll hear a lot of Finnish when you meet the rest of John's family. Finglish, anyway. None of us have been to Finland, but his father immigrated from there, so he still speaks the language and there are old timers here, like Matt the shoemaker. He has a shop downtown here in Rudyard, and he prefers to speak Finnish," Elias said.

"The Finns like to stick together. If you hang around John, you will meet plenty of Finns, including his extended family and of course his sisters," Leena said with emphasis. "They can be a handful."

"Hey, those are my sisters you're talking about," John laughed. "They can cause a raucous, though, especially when they are all together."

"Darn force of nature if you asked me. Bossy, too," Leena added. "Beware, Ruth. You need to keep on your toes when you meet those ladies." The three of them burst out laughing. Even as she felt her stomach lurch wondering about John's sisters, Ruth joined in laughing so hard tears flowed down her face.

How good to laugh, Ruth thought.

After the hearty breakfast, they crammed into Elias's car at about eight o'clock as the sun rose. He drove carefully through the woods, seemingly in no hurry to get anywhere. John sat up front next to Elias, while Leena and Ruth squeezed into the back. "So the women can talk," Leena explained.

After riding with Anna, who always drove, and Eddie and Mary, who always sat together, Ruth found the habit of segregating the men from the women very old fashioned, but Ruth liked Leena and they easily settled into a comfortable conversation.

"You doing okay?" Elias asked, looking at her through the rearview mirror. "You look a little green. Leena! John! Put out those damn cigarettes. Can't you go without a cigarette for an hour? Between the smoke and this slippery road, Ruth is getting car sick. Ruth, crack that window a bit to let the smoke out, and I'll crack mine so we can get some clean air in here."

"Sorry. I'm surprised you don't smoke like John, having been in the Army and all," Leena said, embarrassed.

"I tried but I never cared for it. The Army issued cigarettes to all of us, whether we wanted them or not, but I gave mine to my friends who never seemed to have enough. They were also good trading material."

"I would have taken all your rations, if I had been there," John said, grinning.

Elias pulled off to the side of the road next to a stretch of tamarack trees, now orange and faking their death until they would turn green again in the spring. John and Elias got out to shovel a space for the car. Then, they searched in the snow for a toboggan sled near a tree marked up high with a red dot. They loaded the sled with food and gear. Everyone put on snowshoes. John took the lead pulling the toboggan to break the quarter mile trail. Ruth followed behind Elias and Leena, enjoying the physical exertion of the walk and the fresh air.

Ruth had adjusted the leather harnesses on the snowshoe to fit her boots snugly, so they would not fall off when she walked. The leather felt stiff and cold on her bare hands as she cinched each boot. She had not snowshoed for several years, and she felt excited but clumsy. After walking a few minutes, she felt out of breath from lifting the heavy wooden frames until she found her stride. The snowshoes made a rhythmic sound as she walked through a layer of soft snow on a crunchy underlayer of packed ice.

I'm out of practice, Ruth thought as she fell behind Leena, who also looked out of breath, *but it feels so good to be outside in the woods.*

The narrow pathway looked wide enough for one car. Trees bordered the sides of the road until they came to a small clearing where the cabin stood next to a thick stand of pine trees. By the time Leena and Ruth reached the cabin, the men had offloaded the sled. Elias started the cabin woodstove, as John checked the pipes and fittings for any breaks, before priming the pump in the kitchen.

Without a word, the men left the cabin to walk over to a small building covered in graying cedar shake shingles. It was set up high on cinder blocks, near what Ruth concluded must be the water's edge, now frozen over and buried in deep snow. Ruth and Leena unpacked the food and started organizing things.

"We come down here often," Leena said as they worked. "We stayed here last weekend, so everything should be fine. Sometimes mice and squirrels get in if we leave the cabin unattended for too long. They can sure make a mess. It's best to come here regularly, but it's getting harder for both of us to haul things in and out during the winter."

Ruth looked around the rectangular cabin. One small bedroom had been created opposite the kitchen, forming an open L-shaped living room and kitchen area. Windows filled the wall facing the water.

The furniture included a pine loveseat and matching chairs with evergreen colored padded seat covers tied at the corners. An extra bed stood folded in a corner. A mix of pleasing wood paneling and logs covered the walls. The floor appeared to be wood painted gray, with a large square of gray linoleum in the kitchen. "You and me, Ruth, will stay in that bedroom. Elias and John will bunk out here."

Before she could respond, Leena asked as she pulled out a silver coffee pot and coffee grounds from the cupboard, "Do you know how to make coffee on a wood stove?"

"I can boil coffee if that is what you mean. I usually put in an eggshell to absorb some of the acid," Ruth answered.

Leena smiled. "Sounds like you know your way. Have at it. John primed the pump so you just have to pull on that handle and the water should flow. It's the best water you'll ever have. I guarantee it."

As they sat drinking coffee at a large table of rough oak, Ruth looked out the side window toward the sauna, wondering what Elias and John were doing.

"They are working on the wood pile, I expect," Leena said, as if reading her mind. "We usually keep a large pile of wood inside the sauna, but we let it get too low, so John will be digging in the snow and passing logs to Elias to stack inside. There is always a lot of work to do around here and we always appreciate John's help. We never had kids and John is much younger than us, oh, fifteen years, I expect, so he helps when he can. He has always been close to Elias."

"Are you from Rudyard, too?" Ruth asked.

"Oh, no. I'm a city gal. I met Elias in Detroit in the 1930s. He went down there looking for a job, but found none, so he came back up here to keep farming. I'll tell you one thing, when times are bad and food is short, it pays to be on a farm, that's for sure. Anyway, he found me down there, and we married, and he brought me back here."

"Just like that?" Ruth asked astonished.

"Just like that. When you know you've got the right match, why wait around, eh?" Leena asked.

"I guess that's right," Ruth said, feeling embarrassed. "When do you think we will we go ice fishing?" Ruth angled the subject away from a quick courtship and marriage.

"I don't think that will happen today. Do you see the wind picking up across the ice? You can't see far beyond the shoreline and we don't have a line out to the shack. We won't go out if we can't see, it can be too dangerous. But no matter. We'll play cards and listen to the radio. Have you had a sauna before?"

Ruth shook her head.

"We will take it easy on the heat, then. You and I will go in together and the boys will go in later after it gets good and hot," Leena said. Ruth had heard that couples went into the sauna together, but it was clear to Ruth that Leena would ensure no monkey business between John and Ruth, especially on their first date.

"Oh, I almost forgot. I have fresh *pulla*," Leena said taking out neatly cut pieces of a bread that smelled of cinnamon and cardamom and placing them on a plate in the middle of the table, while she put out small plates, butter, and silverware.

"We can't drink our coffee without a little something. Here's some cinnamon toast, too. It's just dried bread with cinnamon and sugar on top. I used to make it, but now it's easier to buy it at the Co-op in Rudyard. I also have fresh cheese curds from the dairy. Both are good for dunking in your coffee," Leena said as she deftly put the toast and curds on small serving plates.

"We Finns like to have something with our coffee," Leena said, passing a slice of *pulla* to Ruth, who thought she could not possibly eat more after the large breakfast, but the trek to the cabin had made her hungry again.

"John said you served in the Army too. In Manila?"

Ruth nodded as she chewed the homemade cinnamon bread, then changed the subject. "This is delicious. How do you make it?"

"I'll give you the recipe. It comes from John's grandmother. She was a hard woman, but she knew how to bake. She could be so mean. If you make this for John, tell him it's my recipe. He hated that woman, but he won't know the difference," Leena said, smiling.

Ruth felt her head spin. It seemed that Leena had decided she was already part of the family.

"Was it tough for you over there, being a woman and all?" Leena asked, breaking into Ruth's thoughts.

"We felt safe most of the time," Ruth said. "The fighting continued in the hills and jungle months after I arrived, but we felt safe enough in our hospital. Anyway, we were too busy treating casualties to think much about the Japanese."

"Did you enjoy it?" Leena asked, looking intently at Ruth, seeming to want to catch every word.

"I loved the work. I felt I made a difference, you know. We had a lot of fun, too. We made sure to enjoy ourselves and see the humor. Otherwise, it could drive you crazy," Ruth smiled.

Leena nodded, "Hardship is best handled with laughter," she pronounced. Then asked, "Were you in tents?"

"Yes, we lived in tents. We were in a general hospital, so we also had huge tents for the wards. We also took over whatever usable buildings we found. They brought the boys in from field hospitals and sometimes directly from the fighting all over the Philippines. The hospital ships would pick them up after we stabilized their wounds to take them back to Hawaii and the States. Sometimes they went out by airplane. We did a lot of surgeries. Many needed amputations. And the burn victims got special treatment and extra care. I often wondered what kind of lives some of these guys could have after the war. They were so young," Ruth said. "Oh, sorry I am going on. Most people don't ask me anything about my service. Sorry if I might have upset you."

"Not at all," Leena responded. "I'm interested in what you did. I think it was very brave of you to volunteer. I wanted to join the Red Cross, but Elias would have none of it, and anyway we're older. We missed our chance to serve. We were too young for World War I, then too old for World War II. So, we helped keep things going back here while most of the men and some of the women left. We even had a team of people in Rudyard who watched for enemy planes for a while after Pearl Harbor. They thought the Nazis would attack the Soo Locks, but nothing happened."

"Good thing," Ruth said.

"Yes, good thing," Leena said a bit wistfully. "Nothing much happens here. It's quiet. We like it that way, I guess. It's our home, anyway. How nice that you got to see more of the world, even if it was during war."

CHAPTER 11

WINTER'S BETTER HALF

(SPRING – FALL 1947)

———

SPRING 1947

Ruth knew the U.P. winter ignored the calendar, sometime
lingering late into April or May, even June, as it did in 1945.
She recalled how cool she felt in the wilting heat of Manila,
holding a photo Eddie included in his letter of that late snowstorm, writing: "Wish you were here to help us shovel all this
snow!" So, the long months of her first winter in the Soo did
not surprise Ruth.

Ruth loved the snow but felt afraid of the lake ice, especially during the periodic thaw throughout the winter. She
knew her fear had developed when she witnessed a small
boy and girl trapped on an ice floe. It tore her heart to recall
the children crying for their mother as the ice broke apart
during a thaw back in the 1930s. In her mind she still saw
the mother standing helplessly on the shore watching them

drift away. The tragedy haunted Ruth. She often thought of the helplessness of the exhausted men who failed to reach the children by boat. They never recovered the children's bodies, and Ruth often asked herself, *How did that mother carry on after such a heartbreaking loss? How did she endure? Did she?*

Out of that long-ago tragedy, Ruth feared ice on the lakes. So, when John first suggested they go ice fishing she had surprised herself by readily agreeing. With little evidence, Ruth sensed she could trust John to keep her safe. *Only an experienced ice fisherman would go out on the ice, and we'll be on a bay, not Lake Superior,* Ruth reasoned.

She realized the trust she so quickly put in John formed the basis for a friendship much like she saw in Leena's and Elias's marriage. Ruth felt comfortable with John. Unlike Rich, there was nothing phony about John. He seemed to accept everyone as equals, even the rich and powerful men, whom he said, "put their pants on the same way I do." Or the Black people he knew in Detroit and the Army, whom he often said were "no different from us."

Ruth knew she did not feel fire and intensity toward John. She sensed John felt the same. *We're not kids,* Ruth thought. The death and suffering she'd witnessed sobered her, creating a quiet ambiguity toward love and marriage that she kept to herself. But she felt urgency to have children, less because society expected it of her and more because she wanted to give them a better chance than she had. Still, Ruth suspected her feelings for John promised something deeper, more durable than the flash of passions—a friendship that could sustain her for the rest of her life. She decided to take a chance on him.

The first time they sat alone in the ice shanty, John appeared nervous as he showed Ruth how to ice fish.

"You put the lure on like this," John said, showing her how to tie a knot that wouldn't slip apart. "This is one of my favorites. I made it after the war from an old spoon. You drop the line into this here hole," John said, seriously, jerking the short pole up and down. "Now, when you get a strike on your line, you have to be careful the fish don't pull you into the hole because if you go under the ice, that's it. The current will take you. So, if you do fall in, make sure you turn your feet outward and they might catch you on the sides of the hole and I can pull you out."

This made Ruth concerned. The hand-cut hole did look larger than she first thought. She was trying to imagine how she would splay her feet out if she fell in, when John broke into a laugh.

"Oh, you!" she said hitting the front of John's padded jacket. "You are always teasing."

"It's fun. You're gullible," John said, taking Ruth in his arms and kissing her tenderly for the first time. Ruth felt a flutter of excitement. Then he released her and continued talking about fish.

Later, as they ate a meal of perch with Leena and Elias in the cabin, they shared secret looks and smiles. Ruth saw Leena watching them, and she felt Leena approved.

In early March, Ruth had three days off, so they headed out to the cabin with Leena and Elias again. Winter appeared it would never end, as they sat down to a fresh fish dinner John and Elias had caught Friday afternoon. As they ate, Elias appeared thoughtful, barely touching his food when he announced, "John, I don't like the sound of the ice lately. And there's a slushiness during the day that's worries me. Let's bring the shack in tomorrow, what do you say?"

"You're the boss. You know this ice better than I do. It seems fine to me, but I believe your hunches. Let's do it, eh?" John answered.

"Girls, we'll need your help too to haul it back onto shore tomorrow morning. It's been windy, and four can control it better than two," Elias said, appearing relieved.

The day after they pulled the shanty back to shore and put it next to the sauna, Ruth stood looking at water for as far as she could see, noticing it was now dotted with small islands. "My goodness," she said to John as he walked up to her side, "the ice is all gone." Ruth felt a knot in her stomach, as if she had dodged certain death by chance.

"Yeah. Good thing we got the shanty in yesterday or Elias would have lost it, for sure." John laughed. "He sure has a sense for these things." Ruth wondered if she would ever be persuaded to go out on the ice again, but decided not to say anything.

Maybe next year I'll feel differently, she thought.

Later that morning Ruth and Leena sat at the table playing rummy, while John and Elias worked outside inspecting the fishing boat. Smiling, Leena said, "I never told you this, but that first time John brought you to the house, I knew he was serious about you."

"Why?" Ruth asked.

"Because he's never brought anyone around before. That got my attention. I've worried so about him since he came home after the war. He seemed so different," Leena said.

"How?" Ruth asked.

"He learned to smoke and drink in the Army, that's for sure," she laughed, "but, you may not know this, he's always been a thinker and sensitive. I worried that everything he saw and did hurt him, you know, deep inside," Leena said, pointing to her chest. She paused before she continued, "You understand better than most what he went through in the war. I can tell he cares for you, even if he might not say much. Finns have trouble expressing emotions."

"The Swedes tend to be the same," Ruth said, smiling, thinking how little emotion, especially tenderness, she saw in her family.

Leena added, "I think you help steady him, but I just hope he's good for you, too. He's always traveled light, slept on a couch here and there, and quit a job whenever he felt like it. His four-year stint in the Army during the war is the longest I've seen him stick with anything. Don't get me wrong. He is a good guy—funny, fun, and generous to a fault—but he can let you down when you don't expect it. I like you, Ruth. Be careful."

Ruth said nothing. She had heard worse assessments of John from Linda. Anna also questioned Ruth's attraction in letters and on the occasional long-distance call. Ruth knew Linda had helped create Anna's negative opinion of John. She felt so tired of her sisters telling her what she should or should not do, but she accepted the way Leena said it: "John is a good guy but be careful." And she held on to Leena saying Ruth brought out the best in John.

Whatever his weaknesses, I think I can change him, Ruth hoped.

In late April, the trips to the cabin stopped to let the road dry out. John helped Elias block the road, so no one would drive down it and "create ruts I have to fix later" as Elias said.

Ruth missed going out to the cabin. One night after work John called Ruth and asked, "Are you ready for that motorcycle ride? The main roads seem better. They might be muddy, though, so don't wear any fancy clothes. I'll pick you up on your day off, say around ten o'clock, and we can take a ride out to Rudyard. My dad wants to meet you. He lives in Rudyard. I also want you to meet Matt. He's a friend of Dad's and a good guy."

Ruth felt surprise.

"I didn't know your father lived in Rudyard. Why haven't we visited him before?"

Ruth heard silence on the line. "Well, the old man and me, we don't get along well. Anyway, he was down in Detroit staying with my sisters, and he's only been back a month, so I didn't get over to see him yet."

Upon learning John did not get along with his father, Ruth felt anxious about meeting him. *I hope Leena and Elias will be around to ease any tension*, she thought.

When she met Jacob, she wondered why they didn't get along. His full, white beard made him look like Santa Claus. He seemed quiet and thoughtful. And when he told a self-effacing joke about a pair named Toivo and Aino who never seemed to get anything right, she laughed hard, thinking, *John must get his sense of humor from Jacob*, but she noticed John did not laugh.

They walked from Jacob's rooming house to Matt's shoe repair store, so John could introduce her to Matt, whom Ruth also liked, although she could not understand the exchange of Finnish between the three men. When Jacob and John stepped over to a corner of the store to look at a saddle Matt had recently repaired, Matt leaned over to Ruth and said in English, "Listen, I don't care what you hear about Jacob, I'm here to tell you, he's a good man."

Ruth was too surprised to ask him what people might say, when he whispered, "Some say he's a communist. By God, don't you believe it. Jacob tried to make things better for families when he worked the mines up in the Copper Country. Then he tried to improve safety in that damn defense plant during the war. He's no communist. He's a good man."

"Matt, what are you telling my girl?" John interrupted. Ruth blushed when she heard John call her "my girl" for the first time.

"I was telling her what an ungrateful pain in the ass kid you were, coming in here begging for candy and never finishing the sweeping. I told her she should find another fella if she don't want a life of woe," Matt laughed.

After their first motorcycle ride together, Ruth felt spring's persistent push against winter, as the smell of new grass promised a warm, if short, summer. When John took her to the Halfaday Creek on Lake Superior near Salt Point, she felt an instant sense of belonging and wonder as she studied the partially-frozen creek that circled a small island as it flowed out of the woods making its way out to Lake Superior. John said the mouth of the river changed every year, and he had missed checking on it each spring while he was away in the Army.

"That's my favorite fishing spot," John said, pointing to a snow-covered fallen birch tree. As Ruth looked, she saw multiple stands of paper white birch trees clustered around the open area. It reminded her of Big Bay. She felt she had found home.

"We'll come here as soon as the snow clears," Ruth heard John say. "I have a pup tent that we can squeeze into and we can fish and watch the creek flow or go over that rise and watch Lake Superior. Let's come on Memorial Day. What do you say?"

Ruth had agreed, but the unpredictable weather interfered when a Memorial Day snowstorm blanketed the U.P. The blizzard paralyzed the region, as businesses closed early, and cars were stuck, even abandoned, in the deep snows. May 1947 would be a cruel reminder of winter's grip on the north, delaying the start of summer. John and Ruth made the best of the situation, helping Nora build a snowman out of the fresh wet snow, as Linda watched from inside drinking hot tea spiked with lemon and gin. Ruth watched her shaking her head, wondering if the weather upset her or if it was John's charm over Ruth and Nora as he played in the snow like a kid.

SUMMER 1947

Sandwiched between the Upper Peninsula's dark months of icy cold, the warmth of the short summer seemed to create a panic in people to get outdoors for picnics, baseball games, and band concerts in the park. After years of wartime rationing, everyone seemed eager to spend money—including tourists from Chicago, Detroit, and throughout the Great Lakes who crowded into rustic cabins, lodges, and campsites.

Ruth and John shunned the tourist crowds, preferring the isolated spots along Lake Superior where they shared the peace and freshness of the lakeshore. For Ruth, Lake Superior was an old friend who offered cooling comfort after the dripping heat of the Philippines.

By June, when the snow had melted away in the woods, Ruth knew John was the one. She felt her heart jump each time she saw him rushing toward her wearing his leather motorcycle jacket, his leather hat cocked back on his head so he could give her a kiss.

I hope he asks me to marry him soon, Ruth thought.

They had done some things in that pup tent up at the lake that she worried about. Pregnancy out of wedlock would be a disaster, but when she did not get pregnant after their first time, she worried that she was too old to have children. Maybe she was barren like her sister Anna. Maybe she and John would have to learn to live without children like Elias and Leena. They seemed to have a wonderful marriage, but Ruth felt Leena's chain smoking had something to do with not being able to have children.

In early July, John casually mentioned that his seven sisters and their husbands who lived in California, the Detroit area, and in town planned to gather for an impromptu family reunion.

"They usually don't tell me they're visiting until they're leaving unless they need me to do some work. This time I think they're intrigued to meet you," John said. Ruth felt a lurch in her stomach. *Why are families so cruel to one another?* she wondered. Her sisters could also be mean, Ruth knew. *We're both the youngest of large families. Is that what invites this rough treatment?* she wondered further.

Ruth felt John had the added burden of also being the only son, like the daughters did not matter. But if that were the case, Ruth knew John felt no privileges in being the only son. Instead, he told her, he had felt neglected by his father and bossed around by his older sisters after their mother died. They were his sisters, so he loved them, but they hurt him, too, which made Ruth feel defensive for John.

They planned to have a potluck gathering on Sugar Island at his sister's farm. They also invited friends on the island and other relatives from the area, so the day promised to be filled with strangers. Ruth felt nervous and outnumbered, but Leena, Elias, and Jacob—who spent part of each summer helping Finnish farmers on the Island—would be there as well, and Linda and Nora were coming, which gave Ruth a sense of comfort.

On the day of the party, Elias and Leena picked them up to take them over to Sugar Island. But at the last minute, Linda decided not to go, claiming a headache, and begging off in case she got sick in the crowded car. She handed over her baked blueberry and apple pies to Ruth to take to the party.

"You go and have a good time. I'll stay here with Nora," she said, but the latter was disappointed not to see a farm, which John had told her had chickens, pigs, and horses.

"Why don't you let Nora come with us?" Ruth asked Linda.

"Oh, no. I don't want her running around a filthy farm. She might bring back cow manure on her shoes or get hurt on the farm equipment. Besides, they have an outhouse, you said. I don't want her exposed to that."

Ruth sighed. Linda had never been adventurous, and she understood Linda probably never intended to go. *At least she made the pies. But why does she have to limit what Nora can experience?* Ruth wondered. *She always acts like she cannot trust me, that I might influence Nora the wrong way,* Ruth thought, feeling angry. But she also felt sympathy for Linda that her husband, Stewart, would not come home until after the first of the year when, he told Linda, a position at the Coast Guard station would open.

As they waited in line for the ferry to the Sugar Island side, Elias said, "You know, only recently they used to travel back and forth by canoes and small boats at different places along the river."

"Now, Elias, quit pulling Ruth's leg. You know they got regular ferry service here in the late 1920s!" Leena turned to Ruth and warned, "That reminds me, when these damn Finns get together drinking and talking, they spin tales. You have to take everything they say with a grain of salt."

"Hey, old lady, I am not telling lies. I just got off track by a few decades," Elias yelled to her in the back seat, laughing, as John joined in.

"You old fool."

After crossing the river, Elias drove slowly off the ferry and straight ahead over bridges until he approached the bottom of a steep hill, when he seemed to hesitate.

"Elias, you'll never get up that hill if you don't give it some gas. Step on it," John said.

A cautious driver, Elias pushed on the gas and the car sailed up near the crest of the hill, where it seemed to lag, suspended on the slippery gravel.

"Keep going, Elias, give it some more gas or we'll slide backward!" John yelled encouragingly.

Ruth and Leena gripped each other's hands, hoping for the best, as the car crested the hill and jerked ahead. When the road disappeared and Ruth saw blue sky ahead, she worried they would fall off a cliff.

"That's it now, slow down, Elias," John coached him. "The road is coming up fast. There, see… Now turn right."

Once Elias got going, he seemed reluctant to slow the car down, but another shout from John to "slow the hell down" returned him to his usual easygoing pace. Seeing the road off to the right, Elias turned onto a sandy trail leading into the farm property. The road dead-ended at a grey shingled two-story farmhouse, with an enclosed porch along the south side of the house to catch the sun.

As they walked toward the house through a crowd of people, John introduced Ruth to so many cousins and friends she felt dizzy trying to remember names and connections. Seeing Jacob, she walked over to greet him. He was talking in animated Finnish with the couple, she learned, he was staying with, who ran a dairy on the island and were said to have the best sauna in the area. He introduced them as being friends from the "Old Country."

Among the blond children, Ruth saw black-headed children with bronzed skin. John said, "Those are Buddy's kids. Come meet him and his wife, Grace. He was also in the Pacific, but he served in the Navy."

As they approached the couple, Buddy grabbed Ruth into a friendly bear hug. "You must be Ruth," he said.

"Now Bud, don't crush her," his wife said grabbing her hand in a powerful shake. "My name is Grace. It is so good to finally meet you. Have you met the sisters yet?" she asked.

"I've met Louise, Elizabeth, and Sophia in town, but not the ones from California and Detroit," Ruth answered. "Oh, I forgot the pies in the back of the car," Ruth said looking back toward the car.

Buddy said, "Come on, John, let's get those pies. I might start with pie if I like what I see."

"Here, let me take you into the house, while they bring the pies," Grace offered.

Elias and Leena stayed behind close to Jacob. "You go ahead, Ruth," Leena said, when she motioned her to join. "That house gets too crowded. I prefer to stay outside and enjoy the fresh farm air." But Ruth saw she wasted no time in lighting a cigarette.

They threaded through an overflow of people sitting on blankets spread on the grassy front lawn, as the children rushed in between, until Louise, snapping a towel like a weapon, barked, "You brats get out of here! Take your games across the creek out of our way, so we can have some peace!" Ruth watched them jump over the water and rush toward the woods beyond like dogs released off a leash.

The house had been built around the log cabin core of the original owners and still had the original wood stove in the center of the ground floor. A sink under a window surrounded by wooden cabinets filled one side of the kitchen. A small living room lay beyond the kitchen, added as an afterthought when the cabin transitioned into a house.

Women seemed to fill every corner of the kitchen as they refilled food trays spread on an expandable table set against the corner across from the stove and next to the enclosed stairway to the second floor. The men occupied the porch, drinking beer and eating from plates they periodically asked to be refilled, or they dropped into the sink, as they grabbed a beer from one of the ice chests on the floor.

"Ruth, these are John's other sisters." Grace yelled over the din to be heard. "This is Evelyn and Irene from California. And this is Elena and Edith from Detroit."

Ruth marveled at the similarities and differences among the seven sisters. A variety of builds from slender to chunky, heights ranging from tall to short, hair colors from light to dark blonde, even reddish blonde hair. They all were light complexioned. A few had freckles like John.

Everyone seemed to carry on without paying much attention to Ruth. She heard a lot of Finnish comments being exchanged, which made her anxious and more determined to learn more of the language for her own defense, so she could at least understand if they said something about her.

As she stood there trying to figure out if she should try to find John, the four sisters from out of town circled around her. Elena, from Detroit, towered over Ruth. She wore a casual cashmere sweater with matching wool pants in natural tones, her blonde hair cut short and styled in a sophisticated upsweep. "So, you're Ruth," she said ironically. "Well, John said you were a looker, and I think he's right about that. I like that wool jacket. It suits you." Then she added, "John says you are a nurse and you worked at Ford Hospital for a while."

Before Ruth could answer, Evelyn interrupted in a rough voice. "John says you served in the Philippines during the war. Were you on the Bataan Death March?"

"No, that was before my time. I went in after the liberation of Manila," Ruth answered. Evelyn seemed disappointed and out of things to say.

"Hi, Ruth, I'm Irene," one said offering her hand to Ruth. "It gets so crazy when we are together. Loud, funny, but crazy. How are you finding the U.P.?"

"I'm originally from Big Bay and the Marquette area, but I like this area, too," Ruth answered.

"Interesting," replied Irene. "You see the four of us were also born in the U.P. in the Copper Country and Rudyard, where we grew up, but we couldn't wait to get out of here, could we girls?"

"That's right," Evelyn said. "I don't see how you could leave Detroit and move up here. If our sisters, John, and Dad didn't live here, we would be happy to stay in the city. Irene lives in San Francisco. I'm in L.A."

"Of course," added Edith, "I don't think any of us could live without a real sauna once a year. The ones in the city, when you can find them, are just not the same as ones with a wood burning stove. But other than that, I think we all are more city than country folk."

Just then Louise stormed into the kitchen like she intended to take charge of the situation, yelling, "Quit gabbing and come over here and get some of this food! Leave Ruth alone."

Elizabeth rushed around, picking up plates and waiting on the men.

"Liz, stop fussing. Your man can wait on himself for a change," Louise yelled.

Later, when they got in the car to leave, a slightly tipsy Elena leaned on the car and said to Ruth and John. "Well, little brother, we say you are damn lucky to find Ruth. You had better snatch her up before she finds someone else! Ruth, it was a pleasure meeting you and I hope to see you again soon. Good night," she concluded, flourishing her cigarette like a movie star.

"Well, I'll be," said Elias. "She sure can be glamorous."

"Yes, indeed," Leena said. "You would never know she grew up milking cows and shoveling manure." She laughed.

When they arrived at Linda's house, John walked Ruth to the door.

"I like them," Ruth told John.

"Yeah, they're all right. They all raised me and Sophia, who's a year older, after Ma died. Especially Louise. She was the oldest and had to take charge when Dad left."

"I thought Irene was the oldest," Ruth said, confused.

"She and Edith are older than Louise, but they're half-sisters, so Louise shouldered the responsibility after Dad went to Detroit. He sent money to our grandparents while we lived with them, but he wasn't around much." John's face tightened into a scowl as he added, "The sonofabitch."

John's burst of anger toward Jacob surprised Ruth. *He's had too much to drink*, Ruth thought. But instead she said to John, "Go home now and get some rest."

FALL 1947

John took Ruth out to the Halfaday in late September to see the leaves changing. Fall was John's favorite time of year because as the days got colder the insects, which tormented him throughout the warm months, started to die off.

As they sat eating a sandwich and drinking coffee from a thermos, John said, "How about we get married? I have a ring here I thought you might like, so what do you say: will you marry me?"

"Yes," Ruth said, smiling. Happy to be moving on with her life.

But soon after this, they argued for the first time when John morosely told Ruth he did not want any children. He became angry and adamant. "The world is too rotten to bring children into," he yelled. After he calmed down, he admitted, "Everything I saw in Italy—children selling themselves for a chocolate bar or being torn to pieces by artillery—I knew I didn't want any. It's too cruel. And now they have this atom bomb. Who knows how long any of us will even last? I don't want to do it."

After the horrors Ruth had seen in the aftermath of the liberation of Manila with legions of begging, destitute children scouring through the ruins and hustling the GIs, along with those poor women, Ruth felt she had seen the depths of hell. But unlike John, who recoiled against having his own children, Ruth had the opposite reaction.

If she had felt braver, Ruth knew, she would have found a way to bring an orphaned Filipino child home to raise. But she hadn't, so now she was more determined than ever to have her own children to clothe, feed, and care for—to give them more than she and John had. Ruth came to believe that through her own motherhood, she made up in some small way for all the children she could not save in the Philippines or anywhere else destroyed by the war. John's opposition did not deter Ruth.

"How about I raise them? Kids are women's work anyway," Ruth reasoned. When John did not answer, she took it as agreement, something they could work out over time. She felt sure he would be a great father as she watched how he interacted with Nora and his nieces and nephews at the Sugar Island party. *Once he's a father, he'll change his mind*, Ruth felt certain.

They had a quiet wedding at the courthouse the following month. Wilma, Jacob, Elias and Leena, Buddy and Grace, Linda and Nora, and John's sisters all came home again to celebrate the marriage of their brother. Anna said she could not get off work. She had visited in August, when she met John, and gave her reluctant blessing: "You could do a lot better, but if John is who you want, I wish you well."

They received a wooden rolling pin that everyone signed as one of the wedding joke gifts. Elias and Leena wrote "use this to keep the old man in line." Buddy and Grace wished them a long and happy marriage.

The day after the wedding, Ruth and John went on his motorcycle to Marquette and Big Bay, where John met Eddie and Mary for the first time. Eddie had arranged a cabin for them for a couple of days, and they enjoyed walking in the woods and along the lake before they headed up to the Keweenaw Peninsula to camp.

As they sat next to each other at their campfire cooking hotdogs, John noticed Northern lights low in the sky,]. "Look at that," he said. "That's got to be good luck, don't you think?"

Ruth smiled as she looked up at the Milky Way beyond the flashing lights. "Yes," she said. "It has to be."

CHAPTER 12

FAMILY HOPES

(MAY 1948 – MAY 1952)

——

MAY 1948

Ruth stomped her way home. Each strike of her boots threw up a burst of brown slush against her white stockings and the hem of her uniform. She hoped the long walk home from the hospital would cool her down. Instead, she felt her anger build with each step closer to their rented house near the corner of Five Mile Road.

The conversation with Mrs. Baker replayed in her head:

Mrs. Salonen, you're starting to show. We can't have women in your condition working in the hospital. They don't like it, Mrs. Baker had said.

Who doesn't? Ruth asked, knowing full well the head of the hospital, a retired surgeon, vocally opposed pregnant women working, forcing them out as soon as possible "for their own good," he often said.

Ruth thought he would go further if he could. She once overheard him saying, *It is unnatural for women to work like they did at the tannery, making military boots during the war. Worse,* he added with a sneer, *they never should have allowed women into the military.* If there were more male nurses, Ruth thought, they would all be replaced.

Ruth slammed the front door, rattling the windows as she entered the house. John sat close to the radio listening to a Detroit Tigers baseball game—sacred time not to be interrupted—but when he saw her dirty uniform and shoes, he turned off the radio. "What the hell happened? You look like you want to kill someone!"

Ruth stood there shaking her finger at John, a proxy for the source of her anger. "You know, I have worked all my life. I started working at sixteen, knitting and cleaning my fingers raw for rich bitches in Marquette. Working for pennies! I've worked as a nurse since 1941 when I started training and they put us to work in the hospital during that epidemic. And I served this country during war, while that sonofabitch sat on his ass safe and sound here in the Soo. I'll be damned if that bastard can tell me I can't work now because I'm four months pregnant!" she screamed.

"Ruth, Ruth, Ruth, honey, calm down. You don't swear. Here sit down and have something to drink," John said, quickly grabbing a cold bottle of Squirt, Ruth's favorite, from the refrigerator. He popped the cap and placed it in front of her. "It's the way things are, you know?"

"It's not right," she told John. "Women have always worked pregnant. My mother never stopped working until the day she died, not through pregnancy, not through cancer. It's ignorance. And we need the money. I want our child to have more than we did. You know how poor we both were.

You didn't even have a teddy bear when you were a kid. It's not right."

"Ruth, don't fuss. I've been working steady. There is always an odd job around here for a strong back. I can start driving a truck if I need to. Anyway, they tell me I'm the one who's supposed to support the family now that the war is over so we can get back to normal," John said, reciting what he'd read and heard since the war ended. "Your sister Linda doesn't work. Most of my sisters don't work."

Ruth flashed him an angry look. "They are not trained nurses." Ruth hated it that her three years of study to become a nurse and her years of experience could be so easily dismissed and demeaned as nothing, especially by John who knew what nurses had done during the war in Europe.

John replied, "Maybe you can go back to nursing after you have the baby."

"You don't understand," Ruth said crying, "I'll lose all my time working at the hospital, which included time from Detroit and the Army. Later, if I go back, they will make me start at the bottom of the pay scale with the worst shifts. I just worked my way up to day shifts. I'll have to do it all over again. It's not right. Women have babies and you damn men make them, but you always turn around and pull these dirty tricks."

"Why do you let it bother you? My sisters don't complain. They like it this way so they can stay home with the kids. They say women shouldn't work. Don't blame me." Ruth noticed John avoided reminding her he'd never wanted kids. "I would be happy if you kept working, but we'll figure something out. Maybe you'll like being a stay-at-home mom, eh?"

"Women shouldn't work, you say. You know as well as I do there are plenty of women who *must* work to support themselves and their families. And I like to work. I'm a nurse. I can't just sit home cooking and baking all day long when I know people need help. And we need the money to care for our child and to buy our own house. I'm tired of renting."

"It makes no difference. They say it's the natural thing for women to stay at home so they don't take away a man's job," John said his temper rising. "At least I won't be criticized anymore for letting my wife work." After knowing John more than a year, Ruth noticed he got angry when he was frustrated, wrong, scared, or like now when he was defending something he did not believe but could not fight. She wondered who harassed him because she worked. She decided to drop it but hoped he could make enough money to support their growing household.

OCTOBER 1949

After the hospital forced her out, Ruth threw herself into domestic work—cooking, baking, knitting, and sewing. She missed nursing, but she filled her days caring for John Jr. She loved watching him grow. John took pictures of him and Ruth, documenting his life with a Brownie camera.

"He looks like a miniature version of you, John. Does your family have any pictures of you as a baby that we can compare to little John?" Ruth asked, combing through his blond hair.

"Naw. No one cared to take any photos of me," John said. "I only have a couple family photos in my Army photo album."

John seemed to enjoy John Jr. in small doses, handing him back to Ruth to feed and change. He did not seem to have the patience to read to him, so Ruth did it every day and night.

Ruth especially enjoyed receiving visitors. It made the days go faster and she liked talking with Wilma and relatives who stopped by for a cup of coffee. Since John treasured his motorcycle and Ruth had no interest in driving, she walked where she needed to go, or caught a ride. If she couldn't get a ride, she called Archie's growing cab company.

One day over tea Wilma said, "Whatever you do you must keep up your nurse's license. You never know when you'll need it and it's harder to get it back than it is to keep it up. I know it costs money, but it's important."

"I guess," Ruth answered. "How are things at the hospital?"

"I'm leaving. Since you left and some of the old timers are retiring, I don't have any friends there. I'm going into private nursing. I'll have steady patients, and I think I'll enjoy the work. Anyway, I'm getting older and having a hard time walking the floors now," Wilma said rubbing a leg she had injured during the war. Ruth noticed Wilma was gaining weight, probably because she couldn't walk as much.

Ruth felt sad knowing Wilma and other friends were leaving the hospital. It had taken her several months to feel comfortable there and she dreaded starting all over again. *I'll worry about that later*, Ruth thought, *when I go back. Maybe once Johnny starts school.*

John found work here and there, driving a truck, painting buildings, and local construction—whatever he could find. He never seemed to enjoy the work, however. Ruth wished he would find something steady that he liked, as she had found with nursing. It seemed the only thing that mattered to him was his *Indian* brand motorcycle, which he had bought new back in 1945 with the money he got as a GI benefit until he got a job. Instead of looking for a job, however, John had saved every penny of the money the government gave him to buy that bike.

Soon after they married, John had told Ruth, "You know, I'm no good with money. I never had any and when I get it,

I spend it. That's what I did in the Army. But now that we're married, I think you should handle all the money issues, all right?"

"Well, that's fine," Ruth agreed, "as long as you give me the money you make to help pay the bills and buy food. We can't live on my little check."

Leena and Elias came over so often, Ruth wondered when they had time to go to the lake cabin or the hunting camp. Jacob also visited more, often spending days with them. During these visits Leena helped Ruth with recipes and showed her how to make *pulla*, sharing her secrets and those she had picked up from older Finnish women in Rudyard.

"I'm so glad you stopped by for coffee," Ruth would always say, eager for conversation. "When I grew up, we never had visitors over," Ruth once revealed, realizing they had little money and often her father was nasty with drink, "but everyone here seems to visit for coffee. I think it's nice."

"Well, we enjoy visiting with you and John and the little one," Leena said. "Elias doesn't like the crowds of the family gatherings, as you know."

"Yes, I remember that first time I met all of John's sisters," Ruth said, laughing, remembering how Elias stayed outside most of the time, then made them all leave early. "Anything new?"

"Yes, Elias has it in his head to enlarge the sauna at the hunting camp. He'll probably ask Jacob, Matt, and John to help. I don't want any part of it. Those men will expect me to wait on them," Leena laughed. "Say, why don't you and the boy come to stay with me at the lake cabin for a few days, while they stay at the hunting camp?"

"Oh," Ruth said. "That would be great. He's an easy baby. It'll be good for him to be outside."

Ruth noticed Jacob timed his wandering visits to the days when she baked. Dunking a buttered piece of *pulla* in his coffee, Jacob, laughing deeply, always said, "Ruth, this is the best *pulla* bread I've had since the old country. Are you sure you don't have some Finn in you?"

Ruth always smiled, pleased her *pulla* reminded him of a home he left when he was seventeen, never to see his family again.

After she mastered *pulla*, Ruth found making pasties, small meat pies the Finns in the Copper Country adopted from the Cornish miners, more difficult. Louise showed Ruth how she made hers with hamburger meat, and Ruth thought of a way to adapt her own recipe. She cubed a higher cut of beef, rutabaga, and potatoes, added a little fat to keep it moist, and seasoned the mix with salt and pepper: a simple recipe that John and Jacob both liked.

Creating a perfect halfmoon-shaped pie took practice. Building on Linda's pie crust recipe, Ruth made multiple batches of pasties until even John and Jacob, who could eat the same bland meal day after day without complaint, reached their limit. At the sight of another pastie meal, Jacob sighed. He started to say something, Ruth noticed, when John kicked him under the table, signaling him to shut up.

Ruth knew that John understood when she cooked something, a complaint led to good food thrown in the trash—as it had the time he complained about a stew and they'd wound up with nothing to eat that night except the baloney sandwich she threw at him.

Although she missed nursing, Ruth loved being with John Jr. at home. When Jacob came to live with them to spend time with his grandson, Ruth cooked and cleaned, even had time to read, while Jacob babysat. Jacob made up stories in Finnish about hunting moose and bear in the wilds of Alaska with Johnny on his lap as they flipped through the pages of John's hunting and fishing magazines. Ruth loved to watch Jacob spinning an enthralling yarn in Finnish as Johnny replied in a mix of Finnish and English baby talk. *"Joo, Joo,"* Jacob would answer, saying "yes" in Finnish, encouraging Johnny.

One day when John came home early from work, he stood watching Jacob with his son for a long time, then abruptly turned to leave the house, grabbing a bottle of Stroh's beer from the kitchen. Bitterly, he said to Ruth, "The old man never read to me in Finnish or any other language."

He walked outside over to his bike. He had added a side-car shortly after the boy was born so they could go on outings together. The bike still looked new thanks to John's regular waxing and polishing. Romantic weekends at the Halfaday transformed into family picnics, trout fishing, and camping trips, as the three of them squeezed together into the old pup tent.

Ruth watched John from the window. She noticed his shoulders sagging as he worked on his bike. She could tell he was angry by the way he threw his tools down.

She went out to help him, handing tools to him, like she had before they got married. "I shouldn't get mad," John said to her, almost crying. Then he admitted, "Sometimes I feel so jealous of all the attention Johnny gets from Dad and everyone else. I know I shouldn't feel that way."

Not knowing how to reply to his confession, Ruth said, "John, why don't we go to the fish fry this Friday in Brimley. Just the two of us. Louise could take Johnny, and Jacob can always visit his friends on Sugar Island. What do you say? Just the two of us?"

"Just the two of us, eh? Yeah, I'd like that," he said, looking up with a smile spreading across his face, still looking fit and handsome in his leather biker jacket, his blond hair falling over his forehead.

Riding home from the Friday fish fry, Ruth felt secure watching John's back as she road in the motorcycle side car. John only drank a couple of beers at the supper club, so they'd enjoyed an evening of dancing and talking, just like their first year together. Ruth felt relieved that she steered John away from his darker thoughts at dinner as he fretted again about things he had no control over—like the outbreak of the Korean War and the possibility of it flaring into nuclear war.

The Korean War triggered night terrors for John, surprising Ruth with their violence. Drinking only made them worse, but John convinced himself beers relaxed him. John obsessed about being drafted. "Do you think they will drag me back in?" he asked Ruth, over and over.

"No," she always reassured him. "You're too old now and we have a child." Ruth did not tell him she had thrown away a letter asking her to re-join the Army Nurse Corps to serve in Korea. It never occurred to John that Ruth would be needed.

The long, summer days were winding down. Twilight fell around 8 p.m. when they left Brimley. As they buzzed down the road toward town, Ruth felt the cooling wind on her face, a relief after the smoke-filled fog of the club. The rumble of the motor and the smell of gasoline comforted Ruth. They discussed getting a car in case they had more children, but Ruth could not figure out how they could afford both a car and a motorcycle.

Suddenly, she noticed John stiffen as she saw an oncoming car drifting close to the center line toward them. John adjusted to the right to give it more room, but it kept drifting until Ruth realized with horror that it would hit them head on. John reacted quickly turning the bike off the road and crash landing into a muddy ditch running alongside the road.

Seconds after the accident, a car pulled up beside John's bike, now a mangled mess of red metal. "I saw that bastard. I saw him. He deliberately ran you off the road. Probably drunk or just mean or both. Are you all right?" an elderly man yelled, waving his hands emphatically in anger. He wore a battered fishing hat and beige vest as he rushed over to the bike, leaving his car door ajar.

Ruth felt trapped as she lay on her side inside the sidecar now filling with muddy water. Once it broke free of the bike, it slid through the reeds resting several feet from the bike. Seemingly paralyzed with shock, John stood looking at the bike, a total loss, as Ruth shouted for him to help her. When he did not respond or move, Ruth wiggled her way out of the side car and walked over to him.

Shaking, John said to the old man, "Some people don't like motorcycle riders, ya know? They've harassed us before, but never like this." John rubbed an elbow. "You all right, Ruth?" He finally noticed her standing next to him. Ruth nodded, feeling her heart race. John tried to make a joke, "Well, I guess that's decided. We'll get a car, eh?" He laughed, but Ruth only nodded, thinking how lucky they were to be alive and that their son would not be orphaned.

It's probably for the best, Ruth thought, as she looked at the crushed bike, but she could not help feeling that something had been lost with the bike.

MAY 1952

Jacob paced back and forth in front of the window. "Where is that damn boy," he said aloud, adding a rapid stream of Finnish Ruth could not understand. "Damn fool. The baby's coming. Where is he?"

Ruth had called every bar in town on the party line. She no longer cared if someone listened in on her trying to find her husband. She even called the Legion and the VFW, but all claimed to have not seen John. It was pay day, so she knew someone was lying, but she could not worry about that. She called a cab, an extravagance now that they had so little money to spare, but she felt she had no choice but to get to the hospital and have this baby.

Jacob went with Ruth, taking Johnny along. Ruth called Louise before the cab came to ask her to meet them at the hospital to take Johnny home with her. Jacob insisted on waiting in the lobby until the baby, a girl, was born, then he walked over to Louise's house to get some sleep.

By the time John arrived at the hospital with a sheepish grin on his face, carrying a stuffed pink kitten, likely bought in the hospital gift shop, Ruth had made up her mind.

Boiling with anger, Ruth told John, "I'm going back to work. And we are going to find a house in town so I can walk to work, and the kids will be able to walk to school. You never wanted kids. You say they're my responsibility, so I need to go back to work to take care of them. I am going to get my job back here at the hospital as soon as I can. You can stay out there in the country or you can come with us. I really don't care what you do."

CHAPTER 13

NIGHT TREMORS

(1952 — 1955)

NOVEMBER 1952

Six months after the birth of their daughter, Marie, who their
son called Sis, Ruth's heart ached to leave her and Johnny
each day, but she knew nothing could be done. She felt for-
tunate to get a nursing job back at the hospital thanks to the
growing urgency of the polio epidemic. And she knew she
had no choice but to work as John grew more erratic.

Ruth also knew she could not count on John to care for
the kids as he spent more time in local bars. She tried different babysitters among family and friends. Jacob learned how
to change diapers, give Marie a bottle, and cook meals for
Johnny. Linda and Louise helped the most. Even Elias and
Leena lent a hand, and sometimes Wilma provided backup,
but nothing felt right to Ruth.

Torn between motherhood and her commitment to John, she felt an angry ache to see him struggle with fatherhood and the return of his war demons. One thing became clear, though—they could not afford more children. Embarrassed to talk with anyone about it, Ruth decided to talk to her doctor, Dr. Mayfield, the only woman doctor in town.

"No, there's nothing new," Dr. Mayfield said. "They expect us to breed like cows as long as our bodies take it or we die." The doctor spoke grimly. Her own mother had died young, leaving Dr. Mayfield, the eldest, to raise siblings on a farm in Missouri, and she spoke from that bitter experience. Somehow Dr. Mayfield became a nurse and then despite the odds, she worked her own way through medical school. Her blunt talk made Ruth smile. She thought if they had not been from different classes, they could have been close friends. Ruth respected her and saw kindness and generosity behind her hard mask.

Later, when she talked to John, he seemed calm, even relieved. "Two is enough," he agreed. "We're lucky to have one of each," he added, which surprised Ruth, who hoped again John would grow into fatherhood if he could lick his demons and stop drinking.

But they found less and less need to worry about birth control as his night terrors worsened. One night, out of money until the end of the month, John came home sober. As they lay next to each other in bed Ruth risked asking, "John, maybe you should see a doctor about your nightmares? Maybe someone could help?"

John flew into a screaming rage as he jumped out of bed. "What do you take me for? You think I'm crazy? You want to send me to the nuthouse in Newberry, don't you?" he yelled, referring to the large state hospital on the western side of the county.

He slumped back on the bed, putting his head in his hands. His anger spent, tears flowed down his face as he turned toward Ruth and said, "They never did anything to me." And there it was. The haunting guilt welling up in her husband after all these years as he struggled with the after-effects of a victorious, but bloody, aerial campaign against Germany and Italy.

"You were just doing your job," Ruth said, trying to reassure him. "We all had to make sacrifices for the war."

"But we killed so many people, innocent people just like us," John whispered. "I see their faces. I can't even hunt anymore. I keep thinking of innocent eyes looking at me." Ruth had wondered why John had stopped bringing a deer home during hunting season. It never occurred to her that it had a connection to the war. She never asked, assuming John simply drank too much. Now she realized he could not kill anymore.

"You have to let it go, or you'll drive yourself crazy. And what about us—your family—we need you," Ruth said, holding his hand.

That night John seemed to sleep well, confirming Ruth's conclusion that the alcohol made things worse.

But John rejected that idea. "I just want to drink like everyone else. It helps me relax. If I stick to beer, I'm fine. If you would come with me to the bar like you used to, I wouldn't drink so much. Remember, like we used to do?" he insisted.

Ruth sighed, knowing her responsibilities at work and home left little time for going out with John to the local bars to make sure he did not drink too much, but she said,

"Maybe we can get a babysitter sometime," despite knowing her days of sitting in bars were over. She wanted to spend as much time with her children as possible now that she worked.

JANUARY 1953

The first time John hit Ruth, after he'd spent his unemployment check at bars downtown, shocked her more than hurt. But as the hitting continued, she began to think about her options. Should she leave him? Where would she go? How could she care for the kids?

She tried to talk to John's sister Louise, who lived near Garfield Elementary and regularly babysat the children and fed them lunch after they moved nearby. Ruth stopped twice daily to drop off or pick up the kids. But Louise was unsympathetic to Ruth's struggle with John's drinking.

"Look, the men drink. That's what they do around here," Louise said. "Be grateful the only mistress he has is the bottle. Maybe he'll grow out of it. John always enjoyed a beer, but I never saw him like this. What's causing it?" Louise asked, seeming to imply it was Ruth's fault.

One day Ruth shared that John pushed and hit her, never leaving a mark, but it always shook Ruth up. Louise said simply, "Hit the bastard back. Don't let him bully you or he will never stop, and it will only get worse." The certainty in her voice made Ruth wonder if she was talking about herself or someone else, but she did not ask.

The first time Ruth called the police on John, he had arrived home angry and mean, scaring the children. Despite her anger and fear, it broke her heart to see her children cry for John as the police took him away to spend the night in the drunk tank. Louise criticized Ruth for bringing the police into family business and embarrassing the rest of the family.

"You should know by now how vicious the gossip is in this town. You have to work these things out yourself," Louise told Ruth.

"Maybe I will work things out by divorcing him. I don't need to put up with this," Ruth retorted.

"Oh, no. You can't do that. We can't have a divorce in the family! It's your responsibility to make this work!" Louise reprimanded sharply, but she grabbed John by the collar later that week, yelling at him to straighten up, which she told Ruth about later.

"I tried to talk some sense into him, but he said *I can quit anytime*," Louise told Ruth. "*Then, do it,* I told him. Then he said he would cut back, claiming, *a man's gotta drink*, so I told him he was a stupid fool to risk everything good in his life just to get drunk with the boys."

The last time John tried to hit Ruth, she was preparing to serve a beef roast with carrots and potatoes for dinner that Jacob had put in the oven to cook when John failed to appear. Marie sat on a chair in the kitchen watching her mother cut the meat when John staggered in, cursing and yelling. When Ruth saw him, she yelled angrily, "Oh, here we go again. I suppose you drank your check up buying drinks for your buddies in the bar."

Unsteadily, he pulled his hand back to hit her, retorting, "You bitch, you can't talk to me like that."

When Ruth picked up the butcher knife and put it toward his face, she declared, "If you touch me again, you sonofabitch, I'll kill you."

From the corner of her eye, Ruth saw her little daughter staring at the scene, her mouth open in amazement, but she fixed her attention on John, as he seemed to think about what to do today and what lay ahead tomorrow.

"I believe it," he said quietly and turned away to stagger his way upstairs to bed, while the rest of the family sat down at the kitchen table for dinner.

AUGUST 1955

Over those difficult years, Ruth strengthened herself and renewed her hope in John when they went as a family to the Halfaday Creek on Lake Superior, where they avoided the crowds at local beaches. Ruth worried about protecting the children from the polio epidemic and felt they were safe on Lake Superior.

As they drove up the gravel roads, Ruth corralled John away from the bars along the way after only a drink or two as he insisted on stopping. Since Ruth did not drive, she remained dependent on him, so he stopped when he wanted. But she was not intimidated by the men hanging out at the bar drinking. She learned to take her kids into the bar, shaming John and the others who had left their own families at home. "Come on Daddy," Johnny would beg. "Let's go, please? We want to swim. Pleeeease."

Ruth and John had enjoyed the stillness of the Halfaday during their courting and early marriage days, and it still offered peace and a sense of family closeness. Leaving the paved roads behind for the gravel road that led to the Halfaday, the dust became tenacious. It seeped around the window edges and creeped under doors of their beige Studebaker. No crack was too small to stop it as it settled like a sticky mist throughout the car.

Cars driving over gravel roads created a cloud that flowed over the car behind them. When they encountered a car ahead of them, the dirt would blind John. Ruth understood, if he felt calm, John would fall back to add distance between the cars. But when he was agitated by drink or brooding, he would aggressively speed up to the car, sliding across the gravel, to pass the car ahead. She would put her hand on his leg and say, "John, please slow down. The kids are in the car," and usually she reached him.

Inside the car, the dust flew into everyone's hair, eyes, nose, and mouth rousing a cough. The only defense, however weak, was to keep the windows shut tight, until John would feel too hot and open his window, making it worse for everyone else as more floated in and around the car, settling in like an unwanted guest.

Summers were short, rainy, cool, and buggy. Mosquitoes and black flies relentlessly attacked everyone, dwarfing the irritation caused by sand fleas. But near the shore, if the wind blew, it could be quite pleasant. Ruth accepted everything as payment for living in the U.P., dotted with inland lakes and streams in between the Great Lakes, and she taught her children not to cry and not to complain.

A narrow wooden bridge signaled that they had arrived and all except John walked in, while Ruth guided John into the campsite. John would first recon which of the web of sandy roads into the campsite was passable. Sometimes, he drove in easily. Other times, the car got mired in deep sand or mud. If rain flooded the roads, John would maneuver cross-country over the blueberry bushes into the camp site.

It was not an official camp area, but in the 1950s one could camp almost anywhere along Lake Superior. This spot was John and Ruth's favorite since John had found it motorcycling in the 1940s. Although there must have been others who camped there, Ruth and John, and later their kids, came to believe it was "their" personal camping spot and it was good fortune when no one else was there.

Over the years a few campers from Ohio would beat them and set up by the woods leaving their camp area next to the creek open, but too close for comfort. To Ruth, it seemed a violation and her displeasure infected the children, until John would strike up a conversation to ease any tension, exchanging beer like a token of peace.

Its location on a bend of the creek, facing a small island formed by two branches of the creek before it emptied into Lake Superior, made the Halfaday campsite special. Grass and sand covered the camping area and was rimmed by blueberries bushes. When ripened, Ruth would get up early to pick fresh blueberries for pancakes.

Although a troubled man, John relaxed at the Halfaday. His nightmares gave him a reprieve and he slept in the fresh air. He drank less. Ruth sympathized with John's memories of war, but once they had children, she thought if he focused on his responsibilities that the war memories would recede. Instead, he continued to struggle, and she came to hate his drinking buddies who seemed to keep John churning those memories over and over.

"It's good here, isn't it?" John said as they sat watching the lake with the children playing on the shore. "I wish we could just be here forever."

Ruth said nothing. She felt the same, but work and the town pulled her back. *Maybe someday we can*, she thought.

Marie ran awkwardly up to John, "Look, Daddy," she beamed, holding a small piece of driftwood. Then she turned to Ruth, "Look, Mommy. Pretty," she said, then dropped it at

Ruth's feet and ran back toward the shore. "Bub?" she yelled running down the beach.

"What did she say?" John asked.

"Bub. That's what she calls Johnny. She's trying to say brother, so that's what she calls him," Ruth said, laughing.

"I think that's a good nickname," John laughed.

Ruth had war memories of mangled lives, too. *After all,* she often thought, *where do they think the wounded and dying went after the men were done trying to kill each other?* But she felt she had to get on with living. Ruth found being out on Lake Superior a respite from remembered pain, and she lived in the moment—gathering blueberries, cooking over a fire, and enjoying walks on the beach. She collected rocks, pieces of driftwood, and other things that caught her fancy, such as worn, colored glass and feathers.

From multiple waves of migration out of Northern Europe to the Great Lakes region, Ruth saw her children as Nordic cocktails dominated by Finnish, from John, and the Swedish and Danish with minor strands of Irish and Dutch that came from her family. On the surface, she thought her children and John looked most similar, blond like the Finnish side of the family. Johnny wore a short buzz cut, while a rubber band bunched together Marie's hair into a ponytail that flew out straight behind her as she ran.

While the hair matched, the skin did not. Johnny's skin tanned golden brown each summer, just like Ruth's. Marie's skin burned, just like John's.

Johnny and Ruth could sit in the sun for hours without ill effects, while John and Sis would freckle, burn, and peel. Sis could not understand why her skin did not tan. She would hold her white arm against Ruth's asking if Ruth saw any change. Ruth humored her, saying, "Maybe a little tan." She tried to explain that Sis had skin like her father's, but none of this satisfied her.

Thinking about these differences, Ruth remembered the first time she went to Detroit to work before she joined the army. Growing up in the U.P., she felt surprised to see dark skin there. In the Philippines, brown skin dominated. As she watched her skin transform to a garish yellow color caused by the malaria-protecting Atabrine, Ruth began to wonder if skin color mattered.

Ruth learned the hard way to monitor Sis in the sun after they once had to rush her to the hospital suffering from sunstroke at age three. They had come to the Halfaday for a picnic. A cloudy day, neither Ruth nor John suspected what was happening to Sis. Ruth had worried so much about polio, she forgot about simpler problems like too much sun. After that haunting parental mistake, Ruth lathered Sis in heavy coats of Coppertone throughout the day and made sure she always had a shirt over her bathing suit.

Like Bub, Ruth thrived in the sun. She tanned easily, even when walking the deck of the troop ship crammed with hospital units as it crossed the Pacific to Manila. She tanned sitting in the passenger's seat while John drove down a road lined with trees on either side with the sun peeping in and out through the window.

After the family returned from a week of camping on Lake Superior, people at work would ask Ruth, "Where did you get that tan?" And once a doctor who yachted throughout the summer around Mackinac Island asked what resort she had vacationed at to get such a beautiful tan. Ruth laughed heartily at the thought that an RN who worked year-round on a woman's salary with two kids and a husband who worked construction during the summer and collected unemployment during the winter, could afford to go to a resort. But she loved telling people her "resort tan" came from the shores of Lake Superior.

John had learned the limitations of his skin in the sun long before the war, cutting hay in the intense sun of Northern Michigan in August. In North Africa during World War II, he also saw the harm the sun brought to the soldiers' bodies as they fled the advancing German tanks. So John approached the sun with caution and respect. He seldom wore shorts and he never swam—a skill he did not learn growing up on a farm in Rudyard. He also always wore a fishing hat. Whenever the family went to Lake Superior, he remained fully clothed, often with long sleeves. While Ruth took the children to the beach, John fished along the shaded banks of the Halfaday Creek within easy reach of the fish hiding in the dark pools.

CHAPTER 14

RESILIENCE AND ACCEPTANCE

(1958 – 1959)

JUNE 1958

A breaking point came one night when the family returned from a picnic where John drank too much. He drove slowly, trying to keep the car on the road as he drifted toward the center line, then overcompensated, driving onto the shoulder of the road.

"John, watch what you're doing!" Ruth yelled. "Get back on the road!" The kids, who had been in the middle of a screaming match, seemed to sense danger and grew quiet as red lights flashed behind them.

"John, you have to pull over. The police are behind you," Ruth yelled, scared.

A state policeman walked up to the driver's side, flashing his light into John's face, then into the car. Ruth felt his light linger on her assessing if she too was drunk.

"Good evening, ma'am," he said, ignoring John who sat bleary eyed and swaying his head like he could not keep it up. "Hi, kids," he said in a friendly way. "All right fella, I have to ask you to step out of the car. You were weaving all over the road. You are going to have to come with us." He spoke to John sternly, pointing his head toward the patrol car behind them.

He leaned in, talking to Ruth. "Ma'am, are you okay to drive the car home?"

"No. I can't drive," Ruth answered, angry, realizing how helpless she was without her own driver's license.

"No? That's okay. Officer Walker will drive you home while I take your husband to the station. You'll be all right," he said, trying to sound upbeat like these things happened all the time.

He grabbed John by the arm, pulling him roughly out of the car and propping him against the car as the other officer came to lead him away to the back of the patrol car.

"Wow, Mom. They took Dad away!" Bub cried while Sis put her face in her hands. The officer leaned into the window talking softly to Ruth, "You can call the station in the morning and bail him out, if you want to, but it will be expensive. I suggest you let him stew. It might do him some good. It will give him time to sober up and think things over."

Officer Walker strode over, leaning into the open driver's window as if to ask permission before he took John's place in the car.

"Hello, Ruth," Joe said then turned around to say hello to the kids. "Hi, kids. I'm Officer Walker and I'm going to give you a ride home. Would that be okay?" Bub and Sis nodded after Ruth nodded her head. He got in the car.

"Joe? Is that really you?" Ruth asked, her surprise masking her shame. "How have you been?" Ruth thought how good he looked in his uniform.

"Hi, Ruthie. I'm good. Sorry to see you under these circumstances," he said as he signaled and pulled onto the highway, following far behind the state police car taking John to jail in town. "It's been a while, hasn't it? I think the last time we saw each other was back in 1946 when you cared for my nieces after that accident. I don't think I ever thanked you properly for what you did for them."

Embarrassed, she ignored his thank you. "How long have you been in the state police?" Ruth asked.

"Not long. I knocked around for a while. Lived off the land and traveled around the U.P. and up to Alaska. The wilderness suits me. Anyway, after all that running around, I decided use my GI benefits to go to school."

They rode in silence. The scenery flashed by in the headlights of the car.

"John's a veteran, too, isn't he?" Joe asked. Ruth suspected he knew more about them than he let on. *No secrets in small towns*, she thought.

"Yes. He's having a hard time," Ruth said, relieved to talk to someone who might understand.

"A lot of us struggle. Not sure what we can do about it. I walk with my demons in the bush, but they never go away, you know?" Joe said.

"Yes," Ruth said uncertainly, wishing John could exorcise his demons.

Changing the subject Joe said, "My nieces are growing up fast. They keep me young. I enjoy being an uncle."

"Have you married?" Ruth asked.

"No. You know me. I like to wander. I may go back to Alaska one of these days to homestead. A lot of people are doing that," Joe said.

"John's talked about that. He pores over his Alaska magazines. I think it's a crazy idea now that we have children."

"I see you've been busy, eh? How are you kids doing? I know your mother from Big Bay, and we ran into each other in the war, too. In the Philippines. How about that?" Joe said glancing in the rear-view mirror, trying to distract them as he drove closer to town.

"Wow. You were in the war?" Bub asked.

"Yes. I was. And so was your mother. Isn't that something?"

"Girls can't be soldiers. My Dad was in the war," Bub said defensively.

"Mommy was a soldier?" Sis asked, excited.

"She sure was. She was an Army nurse. She cared for a lot of people," Joe said.

"Like Mommy does at the hospital," Sis said.

"That's right. And she takes care of you, too, I'll bet when you take a spill," Joe answered.

"And Daddy, too," Sis said.

As Joe pulled their car into the driveway, he said, "Look, Ruth. I'm pretty sure John will lose his license. You really should think about getting a driver's license and driving yourself. Plenty of women do it. I know men tease women about driving, but they are great drivers. I think you should take some lessons and get out on the road. It will give you and the kids some independence." Ruth nodded, as she thought about what she would do.

A week later when John came back from jail, Ruth stood with her arms crossed at the back door, barring his way. She watched him as he studied a box stuffed with his clothes, shaver, and toothbrush sitting on the bottom step.

"You're not coming in here. Go stay with your sisters or your drinking buddies. Take your stuff and get out or I'll call the police. I don't want to see you here!"

After a couple of days, John's sisters intervened, urging Ruth to forgive him and let him return home. They noted he had not had a drink in days, claiming he had learned his lesson. Ruth let a month pass before she let him come back for the sake of the children, who kept asking when Daddy would come home.

Ruth knew by now that the kids, although still in grade school, were used to seeing John drunk. They had endured disappointment after disappointment of John failing to turn up when he promised to help them put up the Christmas tree or leave early for Halfaday camping. When he promised to come home early, he often spent the night drinking downtown at a bar or veterans' group instead.

Ruth watched Bub and Sis become experts in assessing the degree of John's drunkenness and whether they should run and hide, just as Ruth had when she was their age. Fortunately, John was not physically abusive toward them. He would yell and scream and swear, but mostly he directed his drunken anger toward Ruth, not the children.

Joe had been right: the judge revoked John's driver's license after multiple drunk driving offenses and suspensions.

"That's not right," John lamented. "A man needs to drive."

"Instead of worrying about yourself," Ruth yelled, "You might think about what we are going to do without a car."

John looked blankly. "I don't know. You can't learn to drive. I guess we can ask friends and family to help us out. Other people don't drive, and they get along fine."

Ruth felt the anger rising, "What do you mean, I can't learn to drive?"

"You're a woman and you've never shown any interest in it. Anyway, I've tried to teach you how to shift gears on the station wagon and you just can't get it right," he said.

"Maybe if you didn't scream at me while you're supposedly trying to teach me, I could learn," Ruth retorted, her anger building as she recalled how Anna had done the same thing. "We'll see," Ruth continued. "In any case, we are selling that car since you can't drive it anymore. And we need the money. I'll figure out something later."

"Now wait a minute. That's my car!" John yelled.

"It is our car. And I make the payments on it and I pay for the gas and the insurance."

Angry to part with it, John sold it to a friend a week later. Ruth suspected he pocketed some of the money, but what was left helped her set up layaways at Penny's and Wards for new clothes for the kids for the fall. She put the rest of the money in the bank for emergencies.

The following week, Ruth called around to find a driving program, finally reaching a high school teacher who gave classes to adults during the summer. He had an opening for her in August.

"Do you want to learn how to drive a stick shift or an automatic car?" he asked.

"An automatic? You mean, I wouldn't have to shift gears?" Ruth asked, brightening.

"Not anymore. And they drive just as good as the standard. Is that what you want?" he asked.

"Yes. But I don't have a car right now. Is that okay?" Ruth asked, worried about how she would be able to afford a new car.

"Sure. I'll teach you on an automatic and also teach you a bit about a standard in case you need it. I have cars, so you don't need your own," he answered. Ruth thought he sounded nice, maybe even patient—the kind of person who might be able to teach her how to drive.

AUGUST 1958

Learning to drive was one challenge for Ruth. What to do about John was another. After his arrest, his sisters formed a line of resistance. Louise took the lead, arguing that "boys will be boys, and you just have to put up with them."

Ruth's sisters, Anna in Tulsa, and Linda, who had moved away near Detroit, united in opposition against John, arguing that Ruth should get rid of him and offering places to stay until she could resettle. Neither of them said "I told you so" out loud, but Ruth felt their judgment.

Anna offered to send Ruth money to come visit, so Ruth took her vacation time that they would normally spend up at the lake to take the kids by train from the Soo to Tulsa via Milwaukee to think about what she should. She did not ask John to come. She just told him they were going. If he knew she was thinking about divorcing him, he did not say anything.

Ruth thought the trip would be a good chance for the kids to see some of the world and for her to reflect on the future. As bad as things had been, Ruth knew they'd also had good times. She had made a "for better or worse" promise that was not easy for her to break. But she needed to think, away from John.

The train trip challenged Ruth to care for two kids alone. Both walked on their own, but Sis at six years old had difficulty getting on and off the train and carrying anything more than her pink kitten, the one John gave her as a baby. Now gray, the sawdust stuffed animal embarrassed Ruth. Her attempts to wash away the dirt only made it worse. *People will think we're poor, or I'm an irresponsible mother*, she thought, but Sis would not part with it.

At the Milwaukee transfer, Sis was fast asleep. Ruth could not wake her or carry her and their luggage. A strange man, stepped forward offering, "Here, let me help you." He carried Sis off the train, while the porter helped removed their luggage with Bub trying to help him.

"You are mighty brave to be traveling across the country by yourself with two children, ma'am," the porter said as he set her luggage down and went back on the train. "Good luck," he added with a full smile. "It'll be fine."

Off the train, Sis woke up grumpy. But she perked up when Bub said, "look at that" as they noticed the ground, covered with a plague of grasshoppers.

Ruth wanted to scream, instead she simply said, "Oh, those are just grasshoppers; they won't bother you."

As Sis walked along next to Ruth, Bub bounded ahead, saying hi to anyone he saw. He stopped to study a Black man polishing a pile of shoes.

Bub asked the man a stream of questions, "Are those your shoes? Why are you polishing them? Do you like to polish? Do you like grasshoppers?" until Ruth said, "Bub, leave the man alone. We have another train to catch. Come on."

Fortunately, it was the middle of the night, so there were few passengers around. Ruth herded Bub and Sis along until they reached a noisy wooden escalator. Bub bounded up, thrilled by its movement, came back down and did it again, while Ruth tried to get Sis to step onto the escalator, but she would not budge.

An attendant saw Ruth's problem and stopped the escalator so Sis could get on, then he ran to the top and stopped it again so she could get off without falling. Now that she understood how it worked, Sis thought it was fun and wanted to do it again like her brother. But Ruth had had enough, her irritation and frustration combining into a rebuke that made her daughter cry.

Oh, what a horrible mother I am, Ruth thought.

But Sis, a sensitive soul who sometimes acted like an old lady, seemed to realize she had caused trouble for her mother. She cuddled close to her mother on the train and apologized, "Sorry, Mommy," which made Ruth cry. It had been such a long day, and such a trying year.

The visit opened Ruth's eyes to the kind of things her children could not experience in the Soo—fine restaurants, museums, and other educational amusements, like a zoo with snakes and animals they did not have in Michigan. And the children loved to wander through Will Rogers' Claremore home filled with cowboy paraphernalia.

But the children missed home, John, and Lake Superior. "When are we going home?" they badgered. "Is Daddy coming? Can we go camping when we get home?" Ruth also missed the northern air as they wilted under the heat of the Oklahoma summer.

During the visit John called several times, sounding sober and asking for forgiveness. "Look, Ruth," he said, "I'm staying sober. I haven't had a drink since you left. I am working too and I'm saving the money for you. I am trying to do better."

"Have you been sleeping?" Ruth asked.

"Yes," he answered. "I wake up refreshed since I quit drinking." He spoke like he had just made an important discovery.

"When are you coming home?" was how he always ended their calls. And Ruth remained evasive, still deciding whether and when to go back.

Anna and her husband, Frank, were over fifty and the age difference between Ruth, still in her thirties, and Anna seemed to widen. They knew what they knew, and often criticized new things. Worse, they drank heavily: evening cocktails that reflected a higher class and more money, but in Ruth's mind were no different than drinking beer in a bar. The results were the same.

Ruth realized this was no better a place for her or her children no matter how much more money she could make at a local hospital. The move would not simplify her life. She would just be replacing one set of problems with another, and it made her sad to see how Anna had transformed into their father with time, including the nasty streak that emerged when she drank. Ruth decided it was time to go home to John, come what may.

Ruth felt her promise to stay with John for better or worse when she married him defined who she was. She also considered the daunting challenges for a single mother in the 1950s in small-town America, where gossip and family could torment you with whispers and harping about what you should or should not do. And she was not confident she could make it on her salary alone.

Ruth did not know if she was too cowardly to divorce John, or too stubborn to quit the marriage. As for love, she was no longer sure what was love and what was habit. All John's promises to quit drinking had come to nothing. This time might prove no different.

There was always someone—a drinking buddy or even a family member—willing to ply John with drink when he tried to quit. It seemed these people, who Ruth grew to hate, delighted in degrading John. Somehow, she suspected, it built up their self-image, even though many also drank.

She would go home and try again, she decided. But this time, she would learn to drive and find a way to save more money and pay off their debts.

When they left, Anna gave Ruth an envelope with money for the trip back and extra for a divorce lawyer. "You need to leave him, Ruthie. You can still find a good man and start over," Anna said as she gave Ruth a final hug.

Frank seemed more sympathetic. He liked John and enjoyed the times he'd spent with him during visits playing cribbage. Frank was a gambler who cheated at cards if he could get away with it. But John was too quick counting the cards, so Frank seldom bested him, which Frank respected.

"Ruth, whatever you do. Do what you think is right for you and the kids. Don't listen to your sisters or John's. Make your own decision. You're the one who has to live with it," he whispered to her at the train station as they saw her off.

When they arrived in the Soo, John met them at the train depot across from the Soo Locks. He held a bouquet of flowers for Ruth, smiling. *Damn him*, Ruth thought, laughing out loud, *it is always that roguish smile that gets me.*

"How are my world travelers?" he asked, embracing Bub and Sis at once.

"We saw snakes, Dad, big ones," Bub said excited.

"And *grasshoopers*," Sis said.

"That's grasshoppers, dummy," Bub said pushing his sister. She pushed him back.

"Hey, that's enough, Bub. Quit teasing your sister." He paused. "Did you kids give your mother a hard time?" Both shook their heads in unison, as if the idea of causing any trouble was foreign to them.

"What does your mother say?" John looked at Ruth, smiling.

"They were fine," Ruth laughed.

As they grabbed the bags, John took them over to the waiting taxi. Ruth waved when she saw Archie.

John said, "Archie is going to give us a ride home in his taxi, but first I thought we could go to the Sugar Island Ferry dock and have a hamburger—what do you say?"

The fall that year was one of the happiest times in their marriage since they'd had children. Ruth dared to hope it would last. She told this to Wilma, who still worked as a private nurse. She never married or had any children, but Ruth felt she could talk to her about this. Ruth admired how independent Wilma was, taking trips with Navy friends to Europe and even back to the Pacific.

As they sat at Wilma's house, drinking tea one afternoon, she said, "Ruth, I've known you for what, twelve years since you moved here after the war? When you met John, you knew he would be challenging. You married him anyway. I don't know about all that love and sex stuff with a man, but it seems to me that even with the hell you've gone through in this relationship, you two seem made for each other, like best friends, you know?" Wilma twirled her tea in a China cup she'd bought the previous summer in Canada.

"When you find something like that, you push through the difficulties. Who knows, John may quit drinking for good someday. You know that war tormented him. It doesn't make him a bad man or even a weak man. But he is an injured man. And he's not alone. We know many from that war who drink too much. Women, too. You're one of the lucky ones," Wilma said, taking a sip of tea, as Ruth looked past her to the liquor bar Wilma kept well-stocked in the corner of her living room.

"At least that's what I think anyway. Take it for what it's worth from an old maid." Wilma laughed.

FEBRUARY 1959

The alarm went off at 3:00 a.m. Normally, Ruth got up at 6:00 a.m. for work to set up breakfast for the kids, who went to school on their own after Ruth left for the hospital. On her day off, she awoke early to bake. The previous night, the kids begged Ruth to make *pulla* for breakfast. Ruth would make that first before she started on the week's supply of bread.

Baking gave Ruth a sense of peace. She kneaded her worries into the dough, and this day was no exception as she woke up to a freezing house, which meant the heating oil had run out in the middle of the night.

The dark winters were unforgiving to those who did not have heat. She had hoped John would bring home money for fuel from his unemployment check, but there was barely anything left after he fell off the wagon, ending another period of sobriety. She did not know what caused this breakdown. It didn't really matter because she had to figure out how to pay for the heating oil.

She could get more money from the loan company, but she hated to add to her high interest debt. She glanced over at her bread box, where she hid the money Anna had given her for a lawyer. The envelope had remained hidden there since August when they returned from Tulsa. As she thought about what to do, she relaxed into following the recipe she knew by heart after so many times. The step-by-step process gave her the comfort that if she made this bread well, everything would turn out all right.

Ruth knew *pulla* was easy to make, but heat was essential for the dough to rise, which took three or four hours before the dough was ready to be braided and cooked for twenty to thirty minutes. Ruth was grateful to have been able to pay the bill for electricity, so the stove worked. When she entered the kitchen, she saw her breath in the cold, but after she tacked up her old, green Army blanket across the doorway and left the door of the oven open for several minutes, the room pleasantly warmed up.

Ruth began with coaxing the cardamom seeds from their delicate skins into the wooden mortar. She loved to grind up the seeds with the wooden pestle. The aroma of fresh cardamom rose as she crushed the seeds, reminding her of exotic times in the Philippines during the war. She mixed fresh yeast with warm water, adding butter softened by the warmth of the stove, and combining it with some salt, eggs, and cardamom. Then she started adding the flour to make the dough.

Making the dough was Ruth's favorite part. She did not need to sift the flour, so she worked quickly. After she moved it from the bowl to the gray Formica-topped table, she used her hands to build the dough a little at a time by adding flour. At first, the dough stuck to her hands, squishing in between her fingers, and slowing her down to pull off the wet sticky dough.

As Ruth added more flour, the dough began to take form and she no longer needed to peel it off her hands. She put a satisfying mound of dough to rest in the bottom of her new mixing bowls, a Christmas present from her children, lightly coated with Crisco. The design of deep blue with white flowers made her think of the returning light of Spring, still months away. Ruth covered the bowl with a damp linen cloth and put it where the heat from the stove could help it rise, while she started to prepare bread.

After the dough doubled in size, Ruth punched it down and let it rise a second time. Once this finished, Ruth worked the dough into three ropes that she braided together. She made enough to make two loaves that she coated with an egg wash to help the bread brown. She sprinkled a light burst of sugar on each braid. Then, she put them into the oven for twenty minutes at 475 degrees. She checked the browning intermittently to see if she needed to add more time to the bake.

The smell of the cardamom bread began to take over the kitchen. Ruth knew it would quickly pass through the old army blanket, spreading throughout the house, enticing the children out of their beds to dress and run down to the kitchen. The family had been without heat many times before in the darkness of winter, so they understood what to do and would move quickly, even welcoming the adventure of being cocooned away from the cold house in the warm kitchen.

With *pulla* in the oven, Ruth knew she would have to persuade Bub and Sis to be patient as they waited for the baking to finish, and then the bread to cool. Today, Ruth thought she might be early enough that they would not wake for another hour while she prepared the white bread for John and whole wheat for herself and the children.

Ruth glanced again toward the bread box. Anna had always looked after her, and this time was no exception, but she was not always right and, as Frank had said, this was Ruth's decision. She retrieved the envelope and hid it within her apron pocket to have the cash handy when she had the heating oil tank filled.

EPILOGUE

NEW BEGINNINGS

Ruth lay looking at the ceiling of her single room in the assisted living facility. She scanned through her ninety-five-year-old body, assessing the level of pain in her knee and hips. *Not bad. I feel good today. It must be dry,* Ruth thought, knowing cold and damp brought pain.

Ruth sighed, remembering how relative *good* had become. Five months after cancer took her daughter, Ruth still expected Marie to fly into her room, laughing, "Let's go, Mom. Time for a ride."

Off they would go to pick up Ruth's favorite, a cheeseburger with *just onions*, Ruth always emphasized, and onion rings, from Clyde's Drive-in near the Sugar Island Ferry dock. They would take them over to Rotary Park, park the car facing the water with the safety brake on, and eat quietly while they watched the freighters moving up and down the St. Mary's River. Laughter interrupted their silence as they took turns telling well-worn stories of blueberry picking, saunas, camping, and hardships safely romanticized by time.

An aide whisked into her room, interrupting her thoughts. Ruth could not recall her name. She could be new or here from the beginning, Ruth realized.

"Good morning, Ruth, how are you doing today? Are you coming down for breakfast?" *This girl must be young enough to be my great granddaughter,* Ruth thought, remembering days when only her close friends and family called her by her first name. *Times change,* Marie used to tell her.

"Yes. I'll be coming," Ruth answered, hoping she got the hint that she wanted to get up by herself, but Ruth knew it would take her all morning if she did, so she allowed the woman to help. *At least they will let me walk down on my own,* Ruth thought, as she sat recovering her breath after the exertion of washing up and dressing.

She thought back to how Marie would prod her to *tell me about the time...* and Ruth would play along even after she realized it was a memory exercise to help Ruth stay sharp. *What is left of your memory after a life passing over ninety years?* Ruth often wondered. *How much have I forgotten?*

Memories of the easy days melted away, first, like cotton candy in the rain. They left behind an afterglow of happiness but lacked details, leaving impressions and vagueness. Slapstick memories of slips and pranks long past proved more durable, popping into Ruth's mind and causing her to laugh out loud unexpectedly as she remembered embarrassing moments of human silliness.

Searing memories clung to the corners of Ruth's thoughts, dark shadows that jumped out to terrorize her when she let her guard down, like the memory of witnessing her mother dying of cancer in the hospital.

"Take care of my dear little girl," Ruth saw her mother saying to Anna, failing then to understand her mother's request would become Anna's lifelong mission until she died at age eighty-five.

Next in terror came the late nights when their father returned home violently drunk on bootlegged gin, raging with self-pity at the loss of his handmaid wife, demanding Anna fill her place, and pulling her behind a closed door away from Ruth's grasp.

Between the fluff and the darkness lay a bittersweet middle ground of memory Ruth cherished. Meeting her husband John, *my fellow World War II veteran*, Ruth wondered how he survived as a gunner bolted into the belly of bombers he flew in over Germany. He escaped death in shot up planes, only to lose his eye to an accidental exploding bottle of O-SO Grape soda after he came home.

John had always laughed at the irony. Ruth smiled, cherishing the first time she saw him lying in the hospital bed, looking like a movie star with a dazzling smile and his thick blond hair falling back from his face, half covered with a white gauze patch. As soon as he saw her holding a shot of penicillin upright in her hand, he laughed mischievously and said, "Hey, beautiful, what are you going to do with that needle?" Ruth had grown to love John for never seeming to notice her partially paralyzed face, a wound from her childhood.

Ruth walked slowly down the hall with her walker to the dining room, an open, all-purpose area across from the front desk. She sat at her assigned seat, waiting for some oatmeal and half a banana. Although she greeted everyone at the table, Ruth could not recall anyone's name, but it did not matter since there was little conversation anymore. *Each of us seeks refuge in our own thoughts and memories*, Ruth realized.

Ruth thought of the times when Marie had the afternoon free. They would take long rides through the countryside up to Lake Superior, where Ruth would sit in the car with the window open, listening to the waves, feeling the sun and breeze on her face. Marie took photos and searched for interesting pieces of driftwood and rocks to show Ruth, just like she had when she was a child with a blonde ponytail blowing in the wind. Sometimes they took the shoreline treasures back to Ruth's windowsill, but mostly they left them in their "home," as Marie described it, gently reminding Ruth that her current collection of rocks and driftwood flowed over from the windowsill onto the TV stand and end table of her small room. Ruth seemed to agree, but always hid a souvenir of the ride in her pocket.

"Mom," Marie would say as they rode back to town, "remember the first time you took me camping?"

"Oh, yes," Ruth would laugh and recite the familiar Half-aday story. "You were only two years old during that vicious storm, a gale really. I never saw anything like it. The waves crashed back toward our camp. We tore down the tents in the dark and threw everything into that old Studebaker and headed back home. But you made such a fuss!"

At this point, Ruth would give Marie a meaningful look to remind her how difficult she could be at times when Ruth and John least expected it.

"Dad couldn't take your crying, so he stopped to set up the pup tent in the middle of the night and the four of us crammed into it at that crowded camp site in the pines away from the lake. It was the only thing that would quiet you down."

Ruth and Marie would laugh until tears rolled down their faces, remembering how John had laughed too. *Daddy's little girl.*

Ruth smiled now as she dug into her applesauce, a favorite, and accepted a cup of coffee with a smile and a thank you to the server.

Often Marie talked about her brother, Johnny, whom she nicknamed Bub when she was learning how to talk. Ruth's face darkened as she thought about losing Bub to that cursed Vietnam War back in 1968. But she brightened as she thought of sharing stories of Bub's escapades teasing Marie or "fixing" things like the time he tore apart John's favorite outboard motor to understand how it worked. He did get it back together, but it took years and by then John had a new, more powerful motor. Ruth and Marie always confined their memories to the 1950s and early 1960s, when Ruth could remember familiar events and cherish Bub's potential in life, long before the government drafted him into the jungle.

Another useless war, like Korea, Ruth thought, *only much longer.* It seemed to Ruth the country never could free itself of war. Ruth felt it easier to count the years of true peace in her life, spanning from the end of World War I and the flu pandemic to this confusing time of endless fighting against terror. *What a ridiculous idea that is,* Ruth thought. *War is terror. Terror to fight terror only leads to more misery and death,* she had often told Marie.

Ruth headed back to her room to rest until lunch. *Maybe I'll go outside later,* she thought as she walked the hallway back to her room. She noticed the distance seemed to be farther lately and she wondered how long she had before she would be carted to and from her room in a wheelchair. *Damn,* she thought, wishing her body would allow her to run again like she did as a kid. *Wouldn't that be glorious?*

As Ruth settled down into her overstuffed chair by the window where she could watch freighters pass by, she realized how lost she felt without Marie. She spent most of each day alone, thinking—seldom venturing out except for meals and a breath of fresh air. Her small pile of favorite books lay untouched on her end table. Many days, she felt ready to join the rest of her family and friends. But each day when the sun rose, she felt a renewed sense of hope and privilege to be alive another day. She did not want to let go of this gift just yet, but she felt so tired and alone.

Ruth remembered herself in her early twenties arriving as an Army nurse in Manila after American bombers and artillery had obliterated the city, defeating the Japanese military as it systematically wreaked its revenge, fighting to the death. A destroyed city, Ruth still saw the remains of once-stately homes and buildings spilling over the streets. Legions of rats, who seemed the only victors, scurried unchecked. Countless Filipino children, barely clothed and hungry, climbed through the wreckage searching for anything to eat or to sell to the GIs who replaced the occupying Japanese forces.

Broken to tears at the sight, many of the nurses and soldiers entering the city passed chocolate and whatever food they carried in their rations to the flocks of children, until a Colonel yelled, "You can't save them all." But Ruth felt determined to try, and generously paid for mangoes and trinkets.

Ruth recalled so many burn victims, looking like mummies in white dressings from the bloody fight for the Philippines. Some, with minor injuries, mysteriously died at night, seemingly giving up on life, ending their pain and nightmares. But she also remembered one Japanese prisoner, however, had recovered quickly with treatment and food. His grateful transition from kamikaze soldier in service to the Emperor to an obedient hospital ward boy cleaning bed pans, dirty dishes, and sheets, unnerved the men who lay helpless in their cots, the sides of the canvas tents rolled up to lessen the oppressive heat and humidity.

Ruth remembered soldiers screaming, "If he comes near me, I'll kill him," knowing their days of killing were over as they awaited evacuation back to the States. The nurses had nicknamed him, Arrowgoto, mangling a word he repeated daily, learning later he was saying *arigato*—thank you in Japanese. He worked patiently through the ward, with a broad smile on his face. *He must be relieved to be alive*, Ruth had thought.

He had greeted Ruth each morning with a deep bow, which made her smile as she nodded an acknowledgement. At every verbal blow, he smiled broadly, bowing until his Imperial brown hat nearly brushed the ground, as if to say, "I understand your anger. Please forgive me." After American atomic bombs wiped out Hiroshima and Nagasaki, most of the men lost interest in harassing their prisoner, pitying him more than they hated him for the war, and turning their thoughts to going home.

After Ryuo, in Japan's Shiga Prefecture, became a sister city to Sault Ste. Marie in 1974, and Japanese tourists flocked to visit the Soo Locks and to admire the Torii gate that Governor Osborn brought back from Japan to the park decades before the war, it seemed as if the war had never happened. But Ruth knew the odd mix of trauma and excitement lived on in the minds of those who lived it.

Ruth wondered how she could have cared for an enemy soldier, then remembered it was Lieutenant Wilson demanding the best of her. What happened to her, and the other fast friends from the war years, Ruth wondered, as she tried to recall letters and cards after the war. When did they stop? Were her friends also sitting alone somewhere in a home much like this, waiting, Ruth wondered. *Wouldn't it be nice if we could magically be together now?* Ruth thought.

A nurse came to check Ruth's blood pressure and give her a pill. Ruth looked longingly at her stethoscope, like the one she'd kept from the war. "I used to have one of those," she said, pointing to it.

"Oh, really," the nurse answered. "Were you a nurse or a doctor?"

"I'm still a nurse: an RN," Ruth laughed defensively. "I'm not dead yet."

"Of course," the young woman said in a humoring professional voice, uninterested in learning more.

That's the way it goes now, Ruth thought.

Settling back into her chair, she closed her eyes. Thinking back on the war, Ruth wondered why she and John made it home when so many others did not? She felt she survived everything life threw at her, living more than twice as long as her mother. *Lucky,* she guessed.

As the youngest, all her brothers and sisters had slipped away one by one long before Ruth turned eighty. And John, her husband of sixty-two years, left her five years ago. No more comfortable arguments, just the silent void numbed by TV noise. She never wanted to live in this "old age home." She wanted to die at home, but Marie insisted on the move after John died. How they'd fought. Ruth said horrible things to Marie, but her daughter persisted. Only later did Ruth realize Marie's plan; she wanted Ruth safe, in case her cancer treatments failed, as they eventually did.

So many losses over time, Ruth thought, as she watched yellow leaves glowing in the sun as they floated on the wind outside her window. She missed her closest friend, Wilma, her Navy nurse friend who died before Ruth retired at sixty-five. Ruth ached to think about the rest of her nurse friends—all gone—who had followed in the years after Wilma died.

She missed shared memories of nursing, such as the time soon after the war when Ruth and Wilma worked tirelessly together to save those burned twins, stubborn survivors of a speeding drunk driver that hit their family car. It happened in winter and Ruth still recalled the smell of wet wool. And she remembered her surprise learning her childhood friend, Joe, who intersected with Ruth's life again and again like a guardian spirit, was their uncle.

Years later, Ruth met one of the sisters, grown and healthy, as she handed over quarters for a slot machine at the old casino in Brimley. *Was her name, Joyce?* Ruth struggled to remember.

"I know what you did for us," Joyce had said. "You saved both of us. Thank you." She wanted to give Ruth a hug, but Joyce could not leave the cashier's booth. They shared a long look, neither knowing what to say next as a line formed behind Ruth. She felt embarrassed. She smiled. *I'm glad everything turned out okay*, Ruth thought she had said or maybe she said nothing. She turned and left, rejoining John at their favorite slot machines.

Ruth stared at the large TV screen that Marie had given her so she could see better, now muted into quiet submission. *A damn waste of time*, Ruth thought. Bored, she turned it off and grabbed her walker to go outside onto the porch, at the front of the facility facing the locks, to breath in the fresh autumn air. She hated using the walker, but Marie had convinced her it was just a "tool" and decorated it with silly cow stickers that made Ruth smile.

Ruth thought of all the miles she had walked to and from work at the War Memorial Hospital, where she met John, after she had moved in with her sister Linda following the war. John's motorcycle then replaced walking, followed by a fleet of cars after the kids were born.

Once Ruth retired, she and John religiously "took rides" all over the county to count deer or find trillium flowers in spring and multicolored leaves in the fall. Wilma had been right; John did grow out of his alcohol addiction. They had twenty-five good years together without it at the end. Sometimes, they walked together—a quiet time they shared as they aged until hardening of the arteries from long years of smoking made walking too painful for John.

He liked to speculate aloud how much longer he had, and Ruth always said, *You will go when God is ready for you and not before.* Now she wondered how much time she had and laughed to herself. Not knowing the answer, she said playfully to the walker, "Let's go, 'Tool.' Let's see if there are any freighters passing."

Ruth wore a heavy, deep green sweatshirt jacket decorated with embroidered red cardinals that protected her against the fall chill as she watched the freighters. Each boat moved up or down the river through the locks in just minutes. Ruth recalled how "locking through" use to take much longer when she and the kids would walk to town to shop, then detour over to the Soo Locks Park on their way home. One summer after high school graduation, before the Army took him, Bub worked as a boatswain on the boats traveling across Lake Superior and Lake Michigan. Ruth would drive over to talk with him through the fence and pass a care package as his boat went through the locks.

"Ruth," Sally called out to her on the porch. She was one of Ruth's favorite aides, sensible and respectful. She never called Ruth honey or sweetie as some of the younger aides did. Sally lived outside of town and had just enough Ojibwe blood in her to cause trouble for her in life, but not enough to join a local tribe. "You have a visitor. She says she knows you. Do you want to come inside to see her, or do you want me to ask her to come out here?"

Ruth turned to look through the window. She was surprised to see a familiar face that she could not place. "I'll come. I'm getting cold. It will just take me a minute." She walked slowly, steadied by the walker, to the door. Sally made sure the electric door stayed opened as Ruth went through.

"Mrs. Salonen, do you remember me? My name is Joyce. I'm Joe Walker's niece. Remember you cared for me and my sister, Joan, when we were children?"

Ruth struggled, confused. "Didn't I see you at the casino?" Ruth finally said, remembering a connection.

"That was several years ago, but, yes, that was me. I used to work part time there. You have a good memory. Let me give you the hug I wanted to give you that day," she said, sweeping Ruth up close to her.

"Oh," Ruth smiled. "I didn't expect you. Is Joe with you?"

"I'm sorry. Uncle Joe died many years ago up in Alaska in a hunting accident. He often talked about you. He told us how you dumped some jerk officer you dated in the Philippines. It gave him a good laugh."

"Oh, that fellow was named Rich, I think. Your uncle made me see the error of my ways on that one," she laughed, remembering that silly, love-sick girl.

Joyce joined her laughing, then suddenly turned serious. "I was sorry to learn about Marie. I saw her obituary in the paper."

"She fought hard, but the cancer was stronger, just like with my mother," Ruth replied, tearing up. Joyce pulled out a dining room chair for Ruth to sit on and sat next to her.

"I am so sorry." Joyce hesitated. She put her hand on Ruth's shoulder, then she continued, "Listen, I wondered if you want to go out for lunch today for a little break? Is there anywhere you would like to go?"

"Oh?" Ruth said, suddenly brightening, wiping tears from her eyes. "Maybe we could get a hamburger at Clyde's and watch the boats?"

"Sure, that's a great idea. I always love going there and sitting at the park to watch the boats. Would you like to do that?"

"I guess that would be okay," Ruth said, understating her excitement. She turned to Sally, who lingered nearby listening to the conversation. "Would it be all right if I missed lunch today?"

"Ruth, you go ahead. We'll sure be here when you get back," Sally said.

As Joyce brought her van around to pick her up, Ruth said, "I'm surprised you came here to see me."

"I thought it would be nice to get to know each other. You know, I became a nurse, too. I just retired and I have more time for fun things now. The kids are all grown and have children of their own to worry about," Joyce said. "You know, my kids and grandkids would not exist if you hadn't been there after my accident. The doctor told us later your experience from the war treating so many burn victims saved us."

"Wilma Walsh helped me care for you, did you know that?"

"The doctor didn't mention that."

"She was a Navy nurse and I was an Army nurse. We worked as a team with the doctor. He was a good man," Ruth said, remembering.

Ruth thought, *How strange. Wilma never married. She never had children. I never had grandchildren. But all along there was a family here that grew out of that tragedy from the care we provided because of our wartime experience.*

As they drove east along Portage Avenue, Joyce studied Ruth. She seemed far away thinking about something. "Anyway, like I was saying, I have more time these days, and I thought it would be nice if we got to know each other better. You know, Uncle Joe talked about you a lot, but he told us so little about Big Bay and the Philippines. My family would like to learn more about that time and what you went through as a war nurse. Maybe I could take you out sometimes. You could meet my family, too. Would you like that?"

"I think that would be nice," Ruth answered.

AUTHOR'S NOTE

——

I was born into a family of World War II Army veterans in Michigan's Upper Peninsula. My mother served as an officer in the Army Nurse Corps in Manila during 1945. My father enlisted in the Army Air Corps from 1941 to 1945, including service as an aerial gunner in Operation Overlord to liberate Europe.

They told humorous stories filled with a soldier's eye for wry details, like the Army deploying my mother to the tropical Philippines with wool uniforms. Or my father complaining of drinking warm beer at a pub he walked into moments after he safely parachuted to the ground in England, his burning plane headed east on autopilot to ditch into the English Channel.

Sanitizing the horrors of war, my parents spoke of fun and comradeship as they shared photos and souvenirs of their experiences. Until a rainstorm flooded our basement, they often sorted through their footlockers, treasure chests of uniforms, letters, and memorabilia as my brother and I watched in awe. I cherish the memory of their stories from a time when they were young and adventurous soldiers participating in a grand battle against fascism.

My parents' Army service during World War II, and my older brother's Army service decades later in the Vietnam War, influenced my choice to enlist in late 1975. With a college degree but no job prospects and education loans to pay off, the Army offered financial stability while I figured out what to do next. Not realizing it at the time, I followed a well-worn path of opportunity, patriotism, and adventure common to many who serve from small-town America.

Throughout my Army career, which lasted nearly thirty years from Private to Colonel, I came to view World War II in terms of larger-than-life personalities and grand strategy as America became a superpower. But I always knew from my parents that the majority who served were just regular people—men and women—who came together in common cause from different backgrounds, occupations, races, and beliefs from across the U.S. and its territories. Most served without fanfare, and many, like my parents, struggled as they quietly reintegrated into American life between the late 1940s and 1950s.

Seasons of the Birch bears witness to hidden and forgotten experiences of the World War II generation through a fictionalized story of two Army veterans. Like many who served before and since that time, they endured hardships, but like the resilient birch tree that bends under the weight of snow in winter and rebounds each spring, they persevered. After the war, they tried to share some of the magic and lessons of those years with those who would listen to their stories told with humor, wisdom, and grace. Their lives inspire endurance and resilience. *Seasons of the Birch* is their story.

SELECTED REFERENCES

———

Anderson, Charles R. *Leyte*. Washington, D.C.: Center for Military History, U.S. Army, 2014.

Andrade, Dale. *Luzon*. Washington, D.C.: Center for Military History, U.S. Army, 2015.

Arbic, Bernie. *City of the Rapids: Sault Ste. Marie's Heritage*. Allegan Forest, Michigan: The Priscilla Press, 2003.

Arbic, Bernie. *Sugar Island Sampler: A Slice of Upper Peninsula Heritage*. Allegan Forest, Michigan: The Priscilla Press, 1992.

Bird, Caroline. *The Invisible Scar: The Great Depression, and what it did to American life, from then until now*. New York: David McKay Company, Inc., 1966.

Bohnak, Karl. *So Cold a Sky: Upper Peninsula Weather Stories*. Negaunee, Michigan: Cold Sky Publishing, 2010.

Burrell, Prudence Burns. *Hathaway: 1st Lt. Prudence (Hathaway) Burns, Army Nurse of World War II stationed in Australia, New Guinea and the Phillipines [sic]*. Detroit: Harlo, 1997.

Chabot, Larry. *Saving Our Sons: How the Civilian Conservation Corps Rescued a Generation of Upper Michigan Men*. Marquette, Michigan: North Harbor Publishing, 2010.

Chabot, Larry. *The U.P. Goes to War: Upper Michigan and Its Heroes in World War II*. Marquette, Michigan: North Harbor Publishing, 2006.

Child, Brenda J. *Holding Our World Together: Ojibwe Women and the Survival of Community*. New York: Penguin Group, 2012.

Cleland, Charles E. *The Place of the Pike (Gnoozhekaaning): A History of the Bay Mills Indian Community*. Ann Arbor, Michigan: The University of Michigan Press, 2001.

Condon-Rall, Mary Ellen and Albert E. Cowdrey. *The Medical Department: Medical Service in the War Against Japan*. Washington D.C.: Center of Military History, United States Army, 1998.

Crowe, William S. *Lumberjack: Inside An Era In The Upper Peninsula of Michigan*. Skandia, Michigan: North Country Publishing, 2002.

Fessler, Diane Burke. *No Time for Fear: Voices of American Military Nurses in World War II*. East Lansing, Michigan: Michigan State University Press, 1996.

Gianakura, Peter C. *An American Café, Reflections from the Grill.* Peter C. Gianakura: 2009.

Lowe, Keith. *The Fear and the Freedom: How the Second World War Changed Us.* New York: St. Martin's Press, 2017.

McMartin, Patricia Schaut. *A Lumberman's Daughter Comes of Age in Michigan's Upper Peninsula: A Memoir.* Lulu Publishing Services, 2019.

Manning, Molly Guptill. *When Books Went to War: The Stories That Helped Us Win World War II.* New York: Houghton Mifflin Harcourt, *2015.*

Maugham, W. Somerset. *The Razor's Edge.* Philadelphia: The Blakiston Company, 1944.

Meyer, Leisa D. *Creating GI Jane: Sexuality and Power in the Women's Army Corps During World War II.* New York: Columbia University Press, 1996.

Morrison, Samuel Eliot. *The Liberation of the Philippines.* Washington, D.C.: Center for Military History, U.S. Army, 1963, accessed February 9, 2021. *https://history.army.mil/html/books/005/5-10-1/CMH_Pub_5-10-1.pdf*

Nevins, Allan and Frank Ernest Hill. *Ford, Decline and Rebirth, 1933-1962.* New York: Charles Scribner's Sons. 1963.

Nijboer, Donald. *Gunner: An Illustrated History of World War II Aircraft Turrets and Gun Positions.* Erin, Ontario: The Boston Mills Press, 2001.

Perkins, Sam. "Why WWII Soldiers Mutinied After V-J Day" (updated August 2020), HISTORY, accessed January 3, 2021. https://www.history.com/news/world-war-ii-soldiers-mutiny-v-j-day

Petigny, Alan. *The Permissive Society: America, 1941-1965.* New York: Cambridge University Press, 2009.

Powell Township Centennial Committee. *One Hundred Years From A Cook's Point of View: Powell Township, 1904-2004.* Ishpeming, MI: Globe Printing, Inc., 2004.

Rudyard Historical Society, *Tales of Rudyard: As Told By the Folks, Volume I-II.* Rudyard, Michigan: Rudyard Historical Society, 2016.

Rydholm, C. Fred. *Superior Heartland: A Backwoods History, Volumes I – IV.* Marquette, Michigan: C. Fred Rydholm, 1989.

Scott, James. *Rampage: MacArthur, Yamashita, and the Battle of Manila.* New York: W.W. Norton & Company, 2018.

Smith, Robert Ross. *Triumph in the Philippines.* Washington, D.C.: Center for Military History, U.S. Army, 1993, accessed on February 10, 2021. *https://history.army.mil/html/books/005/5-10-1/CMH_Pub_5-10-1.pdf*

Sarnecky, Mary T. *A History of the U.S. Army Nurse Corps.* Philadelphia: University of Pennsylvia Press, 1999.

Stoddard, Eleanor. *Fearless Presence: The Story of Lt. Col. Nola Forrest, Who Led the Army Nurses through Heat, Rain, Mud and Enemy Fire in World War II.* Baltimore: American Literary Press, 2007.

Veronica, Nicholas A. *Images of America: World War II Shipyards by the Bay.* Charleston: The History Press, 2007.

Waring, Betty A. *Birch, Michigan: Gold n' Memories.* Betty Waring, 1991.

Watry, Charles A. and Duane L. Hall. *Aerial Gunners: The Unknown Aces of World War II.* Carlsbad, California: California Aero Press, 1986.

ACKNOWLEDGMENTS

My father sparked this story shortly before he died, lamenting that veterans like my mother were never recognized for their World War II service. It made me think about untold and hidden stories that ultimately led me to write *Seasons of the Birch*. I am very grateful to Professor Eric Koester and his Book Creators Program for their encouragement. Special thanks to Elissa Graeser, my developmental editor, for helping me nurture and knit together ideas into a manuscript. The support and guidance of Brian Bies at New Degree Press and the team of mentors, editors, especially my marketing and revisions editors, Kristie Carter and Alex Futo, and cover design specialists, Gjorgji Pejlovski and Liana Moisescu, helped me transform that manuscript into *Seasons of the Birch*.

I am also so grateful to all who provided in-depth feedback, including Kristin Mitchell Bates, Donald Boose, David Boyer, Jessica Barksdale Inclan, Liz Kauffman, Nicole Lowery, Jane McMaster Merrell, Lloyd Ruona, Jane E. Secor, Maggie Webbert, and Carol Yee. Any errors or oversights are mine alone. A very special thanks to Ruth Kling for her wonderful illustrations.

And I would never have been able to publish without my supporters, including: Indira Ahluwalia, Daniel Alderman, Suzanne Alfaro, Konnie Andrews, Amy Atkinson, Samer Badawi, Betsy Bassan, Ray Baysden, Celeste Beaupre, Kay Behrensmeyer, Brenda Bennette, Bob Blackstock, Molly Blasko, Donald W Boose Jr., Paul Bottrell, David Boyer, Adam Brookes, Melinda Burrell, Catherina Celosse, Tracy Cleaver, Becky Colebank, Tammy Carr Cruickshank, Craig Cummings, Batsukh Delgersuren, Sherry Demaray, Angela Dickey, Vicki Dunn, Major General (retired) Jeanette Edmunds, Erin Endean, Lee Fay, Barbara Fillip, Robert Flick, Dorothy Fontana, Bob Forte, Carol Garrison, Nancy Glaser, Owen Goslin, Sarah Grabendike, Lynn Gramzow, Helen Gravelle, Kristen Gunness, Jean Hacken, Andy Hale, Rick Hancock, Devon Hardy, James Harris, Kevin Haupt, Roy Hinton, Amy Hjerstedt, Linda Hoath, Katie Hogan, Oswaldo Holguin, Marianne Hook, Lieutenant General (retired) Charles Hooper, Megan Huth, Michael Janser, Linda Jarrett, Roy Kamphausen, Shirley Kan, Liz Kauffman, Sylvia Kauffman, Katie Killberg, Scott King, Eric Koester, Thomas Kowalevicz, Rosemary Kukec, Will Lanzet, Jan Lanzit, Greg Lee, Yolanda Lewis, Eleanor Lloyd, Nicole Lowery, Ben Lowsen, Jessica Lum, Karen Lum, Margaret Luttmann, Katie McCord, Rear Admiral (retired) Eric and Marshall McVadon, Jane Merrell, Aaron Miller, Kathryn Mitchell, Jill Moody, Joanne Moore, Pam Moore-Erickson, Marcia Morgan, James Mulvenon, Joe Northrop, Brigadier General (retired) Mark O'Neill, Erran Persley, Timothy Prewitt, Cindy Pritchett, William Pulsipher Jr., Christopher Pultz, Rose Ramos, Susan Reardon, Amy Regas, Linda Reynolds, Gene Richards, Andrew Ringlee,

Lloyd Ruona, Randall Schriver, Brigadier General (Retired) Gratton (Neal) Sealock, Jane E. Secor, Michael Semeraro, Siddharth Shah, Ronald Shepherd, Rebecca Sherwood, Kerry Sheu-Dong, Lynn Shumbarger, Sandrine Silverman, Peggy Simpson, Susan Streeter, Lorraine Toly, Nidia Trujillo, John Ulshafer, Diane Vandervoort, Ai Victory, Ellie Vierra, Antti Wahlroos, Paul Warrick, Margaret Webbert, Patricia Wilcox, Brenda Wilson, Kathryn Wolf, Gwen Worley, Carol Yee, Gene Yee, Nora Yelland, Taly Zion, Karen Zott, and others who wished to remain anonymous.